AF607815

On Biology, History and Culture in Human Language

On Biology, History and Culture in Human Language

A Critical Overview

Juan-Carlos Moreno and José-Luis Mendívil-Giró

SHEFFIELD UK BRISTOL CT

Published by Equinox Publishing Ltd.

UK: Kelham House, 3 Lancaster Street, Sheffield, S3 8AF
USA: ISD, 70 Enterprise Drive, Bristol, CT 06010

www.equinoxpub.com

First published 2014

© Juan-Carlos Moreno and José-Luis Mendívil-Giró 2014

All rights reserved. No part of this publication may be reproduced or transmitted in any form or by any means, electronic or mechanical, including photocopying, recording or any information storage or retrieval system, without prior permission in writing from the publishers.

ISBN-13 978 1 78179 052 6 (hardback)

British Library Cataloguing-in-Publication Data

A catalogue record for this book is available from the British Library.

Library of Congress Cataloging-in-Publication Data

[To follow]

Typeset by ISB Typesetting, Sheffield, UK

Printed and bound by Lightning Source Inc. (La Vergne, TN), Lighting Source UK Ltd. (Milton Keynes), Lightning Source AU Pty. (Scoresby, Victoria)

Contents

Acknowledgements

The idea for the current book emerged during the *VIII Colloqui Internacional. Problemes i Metodes d'Historia de la Llengua: L'Espai de les Llengües*, held in Girona, Catalonia (Spain) on 20, 21 and 22 June 2011. This conference was attended by scholars from France, Italy, Great Britain and Spain, and we both presented papers on the main topic of the conference, the theoretical foundations of the language/dialect distinction. Following our presentations, Professor Joan Mascaró, who also contributed to the conference, suggested that our two papers might form the basis for an interesting book, a suggestion which we enthusiastically took up, beginning work immediately. We would like to express our sincere gratitude to Professor Mascaró for this early encouragement. We also wish to express our thanks to Professor Josep María Nadal, the conference organizer, who, in the inaugural keynote paper, spoke about the mystery of Dante's panther, both drawing our attention to it and stimulating our interest in exploring the topic further. Finally, we would like to thank Cedric Boeckx and Keith Allan for their remarks on a preliminary version of the manuscript.

Prologue

A scientist who comes to current theoretical linguistics from outside the discipline will encounter a fragmented and often contradictory field. On reading Chomsky or Pinker she will be led to conclude that human language is a mental organ that is characteristic of the species, and that therefore it should be addressed scientifically like any other organ of the body, that is, just like any natural object. She will also be told that all human languages are superficially different variations of a single system of knowledge which is uniform within the species, since it has a narrow natural conditioning. In addition, she will read that language is essentially innate, and that the development of a language in the child's mind and brain is more comparable to the growth of tissue or the development of the visual system than to the learning of rules and cultural conventions.

If, on the contrary, the same scientist approaches the study of language from the perspective of the functionalist tradition or, more recently, so-called cognitive linguistics (if she reads, for example, Croft, Levinson or Tomasello), she will be led to believe that human languages are profoundly different, given that each human language is a different historical solution to the same set of communicative and cognitive tasks or functions. She will learn that the structure of each language is extracted from the environment by children, along with knowledge about the rest of their culture, as a result of exposure to stimuli, and that in doing so children use the same general purpose learning systems that are used for the development of other systems of belief and knowledge. She will even read that each language tends to structure thought differently.

We believe that both sides, at least in part, can be accommodated into a persuasive account of natural language. Of course, we are aware that beyond these two broad orientations of linguistic thought lie other, different conceptions of how the systems of knowledge that characterize our species are formed, of what constitutes human nature, and even of what is the very essence of science.

However, we believe that the steady and pervasive conflict between the two broad orientations to current linguistic thought is primarily the result of serious misunderstandings as to the question of the real nature of human languages. More specifically we believe that many of the points of conflict and contradiction here are the consequence of an inadequate (sometimes non-existent) distinction having been drawn between the biological, historical and cultural dimensions of the phenomena we call human languages.

The present essay seeks to present a sustained reflection on how to disentangle these dimensions, arguing that much of what seems contradictory is in fact complementary.

1 Language in nature and culture

Since the very beginning of linguistic thought human languages have been analysed from both a natural and a cultural (conventional) perspective. Plato's *Cratylus*, sometimes considered to be the first essay on linguistics in the Western tradition, raised the issue of whether words exist by nature (*phúsei*) or by imposition (*thései*). And as the arguments of Lucretius and Epicurus make clear, these two perspectives are in no way contradictory:

> As we can now see from the account of Epicurus, the view that language had its origin by nature (*phúsei*), in the way suggested by Lucretius, does not preclude some later social contract, whereby communication is determined for particular societies. (Matthews 1994: 23)

Indeed, throughout its history linguistic thought has been affected at a methodological level by the nature/culture dichotomy, the degree of this influence depending on the period in question. For example, in the nineteenth century, linguistics was often considered a natural science, a response to the spectacular development of natural sciences at the time. The organicism of German philologist August Schleicher is a clear example of this. Schleicher considered human languages as natural objects, to be subjected to the methods of the natural sciences (see Morpurgo-Davies 1998: 196–201). In twentieth-century linguistics, the naturalistic approach to human language was taken up most notably by Noam Chomsky:

> I would like to discuss an approach to the mind that considers language and similar phenomena to be elements of the natural world, to be studied by ordinary methods of empirical enquiry. (Chomsky 2000: 106)

In light of the multiplicity of possible approaches, it would seem to make sense to discuss human language both in natural and cultural terms. The central concern, we feel, is to distinguish in a principled and consistent way between natural and cultural aspects of human language. Nature and culture are so deeply and extensively intertwined in human linguistic activity that on many occasions they might appear impossible to tease apart. Nevertheless, such a distinction can prove crucial in dealing with many of the issues relating to the analysis of human language, such as the innateness hypothesis and Universal Grammar (in the Chomskyan sense) or the relations between thought and language (the linguistic relativity hypotheses). In order to approach these notions in a grounded and thoughtful way, we must first address the relationships between nature and culture in human language.

1.1 Dante's contribution to the nature/culture distinction in human language

Dante's treatise *De Vulgari Eloquentia*, written at the beginning of the fourteenth century, is generally taken to be among the most notable works of the European Renaissance in praise of vernacular languages, works which might indeed be said to constitute a literary genre in themselves (Burke 2004: 65). Published for the first time in an Italian translation in 1529, *De Vulgari Eloquentia* was a catalyst for the appearance of treatises on English, French, Italian and German, in which it was generally argued that such vernaculars were valuable vehicles of communication and that they were in this sense rivals to Latin (Allan 2007: 167).

At the very beginning of his treatise, Dante makes an important distinction between vernacular languages and sacred, educated or literary languages (Greek and Latin in the Western cultural tradition). However, let us first consider in more detail how he characterizes vernacular or vulgar languages:

> But since it is required of any theoretical treatment that it not leave its basis implicit, but declare it openly, so that it may be clear with what its argument is concerned, I say, hastening to deal with the question, that I call 'vernacular language' that which infants acquire from those around them when they first begin to distinguish sounds; or, to put it more succinctly, I declare that vernacular language is that which we learn without any formal instruction, by imitating our nurses. (Dante Alighieri I, I, 2)[1]

Dante identifies vernaculars with the following features (Law 2003: 231):

- given by nature
- without rules
- learnt at one's mother's knee
- subject to constant and random fluctuation.

The last feature here is explained by Dante thus:

> Since, therefore, all our language (except that created by God along with the first man) has been assembled, in haphazard fashion, in the aftermath of the great confusion that brought nothing else than oblivion to whatever language had existed before, and since human beings are highly unstable and variable animals, our language can be neither durable nor consistent with itself; but, like everything else that belongs to us (such as manners and customs), it must vary according to distances of space and time. (Dante Alighieri I, IX, 6)[2]

Moreover, he insists that vernacular languages cannot be fixed in any way:

> If, therefore, the speech of a given people changes, as I have said, with the passing of time, and if it can in no way remain stable, it must be the case that the speech of people who live distant and apart from each other also varies in many ways, just as do their manners and customs – which are not maintained either by nature or association, but arise from people's preferences and geographical proximity. (Dante Alighieri, I, IX, 10)[3]

Moving on to the other type of language noted by Dante, the literary, religious and philosophical language which he refers to as *gramatica*, its principal feature is that it is a secondary kind of language, in that it is not universal: some people in a language community never acquire it. He also observes that even where this language type exists, not everyone masters it, since much effort and time is needed to achieve such a mastery. There is, then, a sharp contrast between these two kinds of language. Whilst one is universal and natural, the other is particular and artificial. Dante also notes that educated language has a late development, whereas the vernacular is the form of speech which is commonly, and definitively, used by the human race:

> There also exists another kind of language, at one remove from us, which the Romans called gramatica [grammar]. The Greeks and some – but not all – other peoples also have this secondary kind of language. Few, however, achieve complete fluency in it, since knowledge of its rules and theory can only be developed through dedication to a lengthy course of study. Of these two kinds of language, the more noble is the vernacular: first, because it was the language originally used by the human race; second, because the whole world employs it, though with different pronunciations and using different words; and third because it is natural to us, while the other is, in contrast, artificial. (Dante Alighieri I, I, 3)[4]

Hence, Dante's characterization of educated languages can be summarized thus (Law 2003: 230–231):

- shaped by art
- regulated by rules
- learnt through formal studies
- unchanging through time and space.

The final feature here is developed by Dante in the following way:

> This was the point from which the inventors of the art of grammar began; for their gramatica is nothing less than a certain immutable identity of language in different times and places. Its rules having been formulated with the common consent of many peoples, it can be subject to no individual will; and, as a result, it cannot change. So those who devised this language did so lest, through changes in language dependent on the arbitrary judgement of individuals, we should become either unable, or, at best, only partially able, to enter into contact with the deeds and authoritative writings of the ancients, or of those whose difference of location makes them different from us. (Dante Alighieri 1997, I, IX, 10)[5]

It is clear that in using the term *gramatica*, Dante is referring here to the product of the grammarian's work, he who tries to instruct people in the grammatical rules required to read and understand authoritative written works. These rules are immutable, and cannot be altered at the whim or fancy of the individual. So, we have here a type of language that is qualitatively different from a vernacular in that it is artificial, fixed and non-universal. In the present work we will try to qualify Dante's position here from the point of view of modern linguistics.

It is evident from the above passages that a clear distinction between natural languages (NL) and cultivated languages (CL) can be established. NLs are natural in the sense that they are typically acquired by children without any intentional instruction and are used by everyone in a language community without apparent effort or difficulty. They are also deeply internalized and automated. In addition, they present a remarkable degree of variation and tend to exhibit a certain degree of instability. This latter feature may give the false impression that NLs are not subject to fixed sets of rules, and thus to the notion that these languages 'have no grammar'.

We can broadly associate NLs as characterized by Dante with what has been called *spontaneous spoken language* (Miller and Weinert 1998). Conversely, formal or literary written language can be seen as a major type of cultivated language (CL) as characterized by Dante. This latter form of language is not spontaneously acquired and not everyone succeeds in mastering it; hence, it must be considered secondary with respect to the NL.

One important concept introduced in *De Vulgari Eloquentia* is the idea of an illustrious vernacular, described in chapter XI of the first book of the treatise. Here Dante attempts to find a specific example of a vernacular variety with the same values and functions of the cultivated language (CL):

> Amid the cacophony of the many varieties of Italian speech, let us hunt for the most respectable and illustrious vernacular that exists in Italy; and, so that we may have an unobstructed pathway for our hunting, let us begin by clearing the tangled bushes and brambles out of the wood.[6]

His search takes him through the many dialects and vulgar varieties of various Italian regions and cities, and although he says he found elements of an illustrious vernacular in some varieties, no single Italian variety could be said to exhibit all its characteristics. It is during this discussion that the famous panther metaphor is introduced:

> Now that we have hunted across the woodlands and pastures of all Italy without finding the panther we are trailing, let us, in the hope of tracking it down, carry out a more closely reasoned investigation, so that, by the assiduous practice of cunning, we can at last entice into our trap this creature whose scent is left everywhere but which is nowhere to be seen. (Dante Alighieri I, XVI, 1)[7]

Nevertheless, he concludes that certain urban dialects, taken as a whole, do indeed present most of the characteristics of the illustrious vernacular:

> So we have found what we were seeking: we can define the illustrious, cardinal, aulic, and curial vernacular in Italy as that which belongs to every Italian city yet seems to belong to none, and against which the vernaculars of all the cities of the Italians can be measured, weighed, and compared. (Dante I, XVI, 6)[8]

The second book of *De Vulgari Eloquentia* is devoted to a description of the different ways of illustrating vulgar languages, as a means of equating them functionally to classical literary languages such as Greek and Latin. Thus, in order to illustrate a vernacular, it is seen to be necessary to submit it to a specific cultural elaboration. This is a crucial idea, since it implies that NLs can be modified in specific ways in order that they be transformed into CLs. Indeed, it is worth pointing out in this context that both Classical Greek and Latin are educated versions of their corresponding vulgar or vernacular varieties.

1.2 Characterizing natural and cultivated languages

Dante's discussion of the eloquence of the vulgar language in his (unfinished) treatise was both significant and influential. In this section, we will try to characterize and clarify the concepts which arise from this, in light of findings from contemporary linguistics.

The grammatical competence acquired by individuals in their childhood constitutes an internalized natural grammar, one that functions as the grammatical core of our everyday spontaneous linguistic activity. A natural language (NL) can be characterized as a dynamic and complex set of grammatical competences. In this sense, it can be viewed as a population of internalized natural grammars in the minds of speakers (Ritt 2004: 98).

It is important to note that grammatical research necessarily involves the study of the internal mental state characterizing natural grammatical knowledge, that is, the linguistic competence of individuals (the I-language in Chomsky's terms, see Chapter 2).[9] The grammatical competences of people might include subsets of identical or practically identical grammatical competences, but it should be clear from the start that a set of grammatical competences is not in itself a grammatical competence, and thus cannot constitute the object of grammatical research. This does not mean that such sets, or the individuals possessing them, cannot be considered as describable objects in the world. Indeed, certain configurations of grammatical competences can in some ways behave as unitary or homogeneous entities. They key element, rather, is that any one speaker's grammatical competence cannot be seen as a perfect implementation or rendition of a common, supra-individual competence. The fact that competences interact with each other in a linguistic population does not imply that there exists a common or general grammatical competence with supra-individual status which instantiates individual examples of that competence (that is, particular grammatical competences).

Speakers and signers[10] are not like performers executing a pre-existing musical score with greater or lesser degrees of skill. Instead, they create their own musical score from the different performances by other speakers and signers that they observe, and in this is guided by the hand of Nature (their innate ability to acquire natural languages). When several piano performers interpret a sonata by Chopin, they instantiate particular renditions of a common score; by contrast, when a group of people speak English (or use British Sign Language), they are not performing a common grammatical score written by an individual or institution; they speak or sign according to their own grammatical score, their internal grammatical competence.

Therefore, if we view a natural language as a population of grammatical competences we are not necessarily implying that there is a common, coherent and supra-individual competence manifesting itself in those individual competences. Newmeyer formulates this idea in the following way:

> There is no 'Pan-English' grammar, one which encompasses every sentence possible in all dialects and idiolects of English. (Newmeyer 2005: 161)

Of course, there are a great many books with titles such as 'An English grammar', but the vast majority of these describe a specific version of Written Standard English, a cultivated language based on an English dialect, and hence describe not any particular grammatical competence as such, but rather an elaborated version of the English language. The natural competences of native English speakers are not instantiations of this written standard language. We will return to this language type below.

Bearing the above points in mind, we now offer a characterization of NL grammatical competence:

NL grammatical competence (I-Language)

- It is spontaneously acquired by children.
- Any normal child is able to acquire naturally a grammatical competence of any NL.
- The performance of a naturally acquired NL grammatical competence is automatic and unconscious.
- It is constrained by the principles of Universal Grammar.
- It is strongly constrained by the psycho-physiological characteristics of human beings.
- Its evolutionary behaviour is that of a complex adaptive system.[11]

We will now characterize a NL as a population of grammatical competences (I-languages):

Natural languages

- They are formed spontaneously in human communities, without any intentional initiative.
- They are established in an automatic and unconscious way.
- They are constrained by the properties of their constitutive elements (individual grammatical competences).
- They are constrained by the psycho-anthropological characteristics of human communities.
- They behave as complex adaptive systems.

- They evolve (change) blindly in a Darwinian sense through variation and selection.

Hence, natural languages can be thought of as products of natural growth, not of conscious convention. Natural languages did not arise through an explicit purposive act of creation and convention by human communities. Indeed, in the total absence of any kind of prior language it would be impossible to reach a conscious agreement of that sort, as Jespersen noted:

> Still it is true that the vast majority of linguistic facts have come about by what may without any infringement of scientific precision be termed natural growth. This is especially true of linguistic structure, or what we generally call grammar. No single individual, no body of individuals, ever sat down deliberately to frame the endings and other means by which plurals or past tenses are expressed in English or any other language. (Jespersen 1933: 705–706)

This notion as to the natural character of human spontaneous languages was also made by Max Müller in his second lecture on the science of language, where he observed that humans do not create natural languages deliberately:

> He can do nothing by himself, and the first impulse to a new formation in language, though given by an individual, is mostly, if not always, given without premeditation, nay, unconsciously. The individual, as such, is powerless, and the results apparently produced by him depend on laws beyond his control, and on the co-operation of all those who form together with him one class, one body, or one organic whole. (Müller 1862: 50)

Let us now characterize cultivated languages (CL). These are obtained when NLs are subjected to a series of partial cultural elaborations that are both intentional and goal-oriented. As we will see in Chapter 4, there are different cultural phenomena from which the many possible criteria for NL modification may arise. These include: rituals, magic, beliefs, religion, kinship relationships, poetry, story telling, linguistic games, social distinction, social power, and social prestige, amongst many others.

All human communities develop some sort of culture and, therefore, all human communities will elaborate their NLs in certain specific ways. These elaborations cannot change natural grammatical competences (I-languages) or populations of grammatical competences (NLs) in any fundamental way. The influence of cultural elaborations on natural languages is superficial, since the latter have a biological basis (in their design and development) that cannot be altered in any essential way.

A comparison with human nutrition might be illustrative here. Our need for food is based on a biologically determined necessity and, at the same time, is subjected to many different cultural elaborations in different human communities. Ways of preparing and cooking food, and the concept of what things can and cannot be considered food, vary a great deal across human societies, yet such cultural influence does not alter the basic biological facts which determine the human need of food or the things which the human digestive system can in fact accept as such (see Harris 1998).

Dante's notion of an illustrious vulgar language symbolizes a cultural elaboration of a natural language with the purpose of serving certain social or political needs. We will now list some of the characteristics of cultivated languages:

Cultivated languages (CL):

- They are the product of certain partial elaborations of NLs.
- They are established by explicit convention and agreement inside a community.
- They are learned on the basis of intentional, goal-oriented and guided instruction.
- Not everyone in a linguistic community succeeds in mastering all the CLs created and imposed by that community.
- They are subjected to social, political or ideological factors.
- They are stable in time and present no or little variation.
- They evolve teleologically in a Lamarckian way.

These characteristics make CLs artificial languages. They differ from NLs in three fundamental aspects: they are not spontaneously learnable, they present no or little variation and change, and they are not usually performed in an automatic and unconscious fashion. These three features are essential and no language presenting them can qualify as a NL. Therefore CLs cannot be natural languages.

In fact, CLs are partial elaborations of some aspects of the natural grammatical competences of a natural language, usually written down in the form of scholarly or prescriptive grammars. For this reason, a grammatical competence based solely on a CL could not function properly as a full-fledged competence. When trying to speak using the artificial grammar of a CL (such as those often learned in primary education), speakers must make use of their natural grammatical competence to fill in the gaps, that is, to provide all those aspects of natural grammar not covered by scholarly or prescriptive grammatical systems. In addition, the artificial grammatical competence learned from scholarly or prescriptive grammars cannot modify or change natural grammatical competence in any essential way, let alone replace it.

CLs cannot be spontaneously acquired: they must be purposively learned. As Dante says, their study requires much time and effort and not everybody succeeds in reaching an effective command of their structure and practice. This is the case, for example, with the standard written languages of industrialized societies. Despite their study generally being compulsory, not everyone succeeds in speaking and writing in the way prescribed by the norms of school grammars. People who do achieve this typically have to make a conscious and concerted effort to do so, and this effort never fully subsides. For example, it is far easier for us to tell our friends in an informal way how we spent our summer vacation than to address an audience formally or write down a complete and coherent report about the same events.

As we noted earlier in this chapter, written languages are a clear example of CLs, and are therefore artificial rather than natural languages. This refers not only to the phonetic level but also to grammar, as Jespersen observed when referring to standard written language:

> The whole structure of sentences and their combinations has to be changed, and even the simplest familiar letter has to be formed in a different way from the same communication if it had been oral. This rearrangement has to be learnt artificially, though much of it may come unconsciously by instinctive imitation of models of various kinds. (Jespersen 1933: 716)

The same view was set out by Müller in his second lecture on the science of language, in which he claimed that cultivated languages will not replace natural languages:

> What we are accustomed to call languages, the literary idioms of Greece, and Rome, and India, of Italy, France, and Spain, must be considered as artificial, rather than as natural forms of speech. The real and natural life of language is in its dialects, and in spite of the tyranny exercised by the classical or literary idioms, the day is still very far off which is to see the dialects, even of such classical languages as Italian and French, entirely eradicated. (Müller 1862: 58)

In addition, CLs do not change naturally, and hence do not originate new NLs:

> From this point of view we can see that no literary language can ever be said to have been the mother of another language. As soon as a language loses its unbounded capability of change, its

> carelessness about what it throws away, and its readiness in always supplying instantaneously the wants of mind and heart, its natural life is changed into a merely artificial existence. (Müller 1862: 69)

Müller concludes by maintaining that natural languages change and evolve independently of human will:

> What, however, I wanted particularly to point out in this lecture is this, that neither of the causes which produce the growth, or, according to others, constitute the history of language, is under the control of man. The phonetic decay of language is not the result of mere accident; it is governed by definite laws, as we shall see when we come to consider the principles of comparative grammar. But these laws were not made by man; on the contrary, man had to obey them without knowing of their existence. (Müller 1862: 72–73)

Indeed, some authors see standard languages not as languages at all, but as ideological models which have an important function in certain types of society:

> Therefore it seems appropriate to speak more abstractly of standardisation as an *ideology*, and a standard language as an idea in the mind rather than a reality – a set of abstract norms to which actual usage may conform to a greater or lesser extent. (Milroy and Milroy 1991: 23)

This applies to European standard languages, such as Standard English:

> Although we have referred to 'Standard English', there is – in the very strict sense in which we have so far used the term 'standardization' – no such entity as a standard spoken language; even so-called 'Standard English' can be perceived to incorporate variability and change. (Milroy and Milroy 1991: 26)

Here the Milroys make the point that speakers of standard languages have to use their natural grammatical competence in order to speak; this, indeed, is the source of the variability and change observed when standard languages are used by those who learned them at school.

In contrast to NLs, CLs do not evolve in a Darwinian fashion, but in a Lamarckian way. Hence, CLs can be changed or modified by means of intentional and goal-oriented actions by an individual or institution with the necessary authority to do so. If such modifications are not carried out, CLs can remain unchanged indefinitely, since, unlike NLs, they are not subject to spontaneous variation. For example, classical Sumerian remains unchanged since it was abandoned as a written language because nobody has used the language from that point in time.

It is important to note that although both NLs and CLs appear in all linguistic communities, the former have a clear primacy over the latter, since only NLs are a direct manifestation of the human language faculty and have a biological basis. As observed by Dante, CLs, created by partial cultural elaborations of NLs, have a secondary and derived status and are artificial, not natural. For this reason, a standard written language, as a special type of cultivated language, cannot reasonably be the main focus of grammatical research.

It is important to bear in mind here that cultivated languages naturalize to a lesser or greater extent as soon as speakers try to use them in everyday life. This naturalization can give rise to different types of deviations from the rules of the standard. Prescriptive grammarians typically consider deviation of this kind to be evidence of the incorrect implementation of the standard language. In the current essay, however, such deviation is seen as evidence of the way in which linguistic performers shift unconsciously towards a naturalization of cultivated languages.

1.3 Natural Language as natural adaptive systems

In this section we will try to characterize the dynamics of natural language from the point of view of complexity theory, more specifically, using the concept of the Complex Adaptive System (CAS) as proposed by Murray Gell-Mann. It is important to bear in mind that not all applications of these concepts to natural language are based on the same assumptions and proposals (for a comprehensive survey see Rosenbach 2008; Chapter 3) and that not all the so-called Darwinian approaches to language evolution in fact make sense.[12]

A population of competences and the competences themselves (I-languages) can be said to constitute complex adaptive systems in Gell-Mann's sense (Gell-Mann 1992; Ritt 2004: 99; Larsen-Freeman and Cameron 2008; Ellis and Larsen-Freeman 2009). A CAS can be viewed as a schema containing compressed information about its environment, constituting a *model* or a *theory* of it, and can be described as a set of schematic rules (Ritt 2004: 94). A CAS interacts with its environment by unfolding that compressed information to yield a specific behaviour; the effects of this behaviour on the environment may feed back on the system itself. Some of the environmental responses may reinforce or stabilise the schematic rules while others may destabilize them (Gell-Mann 1992: 11).

Language acquisition and language variation and change can be seen as particular cases of complex adaptive systems (CAS) in action. Ritt characterizes the natural language acquisition process thus:

> Language acquisition can thus be regarded as an evolutionary process in which a specific part of a person's mind/brain (Chomsky's UG, Pinker's 'language organ') 'adapts' to aspects of its host's body, to the conceptual content of other parts of that host's mind/brain, as well as to the external environment of its host, in particular to the communicative behaviour of the social group within which its host is embedded. (Ritt 2004: 100)

A population of linguistic competences can also be viewed as a CAS: it also changes over time and seems to adapt itself to the changing needs of its speakers/signers. As Ritt has noted:

> After discussing the properties of complex adaptive systems, we have concluded that language changes are likely to be brought about through environmental feedback on rivalling systems of competence properties, incurred via their behavioral and textual unfolding, and that language change can indeed be construed as 'evolutionary', 'adaptive' or reflecting 'learning' on part of the system. (Ritt 2004: 120)

In this sense, Ritt has proposed a Darwinian[13] view of natural language change in the following terms:

> Any property of any language at any time can be explained as existing because it has managed to place a stable copy of itself into the competence (that is, the mind/brain) which has it. This, in turn, implies that the most adequate way of approaching the study of language and language change, is by asking (a) what the replicating units that constitute competences actually are, (b) by what mechanics they replicate, and (c) what (environmental) factors influence their success at replicating. (Ritt 2004: 121)

The following issues are relevant in the study of NLs as CASs (Ritt 2004: 121):

- Neurobiology of language: the material implementation of linguistic replicators.
- Linguistic competence: the structure of replicator systems.
- Linguistic performance: the behavioural unfolding of replicator systems.

- Universal Grammar: genetically determined constraints of linguistic replicators.[14]
- Physiological constraints: bodily hardware for articulation and perception.
- Speaker cognitive and communicative needs.

In natural language acquisition, children try to replicate the linguistic competences of the speakers surrounding them. As they have no direct access to those competences, they must construct their own linguistic competence following the principles of Universal Grammar (on the notion of Universal Grammar see section 2.3). Since they live amid a complex population of grammatical competences there is a natural selection process by which children naturally build up a grammatical competence very similar or quasi-identical to a specific group within that population. This is a Darwinian process: there is variation and selection on the basis of the complex interactions inside a population of linguistic competences, a CAS in itself. Natural language variation and change can also be viewed as a dynamic process in which variation and adaptive selection are two salient properties.

It is important to note that Darwinian evolutionary processes are non-intentional and non-teleological: they are not driven by any purposive long-term project.[15] In addition, variation is crucial for Darwinian evolution: if there is no variation, such evolutionary processes are not possible at all.

Labov (2001: 3–34) has expressed what he calls *the Darwinian Paradox* in the following terms:

> The evolution of species and the evolution of language are identical in form, although their fundamental causes are completely different. (Labov 2001: 14)

This paradox is based on the species/language evolution analogy observed by Darwin himself:

> The formation of different languages and of distinct species, and the proofs that both have been developed through a gradual process, are curiously parallel[16]. […] We find in distinct languages striking homologies due to community of descent, and analogies due to similar process of formation. (Darwin 1871: 112–113)

In establishing this parallelism, Darwin refers to the concept of the struggle for life (a concept introduced by Herbert Spencer, who influenced Darwin) as formulated by Müller:

> As Max Müller has well remarked: ‘A struggle for life is constantly going on amongst the words and grammatical forms in each

> language. The better, the shorter, the easier forms are constantly gaining the upper hand, and they owe their success to their own inherent virtue.' To these more important causes of the survival of certain words, mere novelty and fashion may be added; for there is in the mind of man a strong love for the slight changes in all things. The survival or preservation of certain favoured words in the struggle for existence is natural selection. (Darwin 1871: 113)

Müller, then, sees linguistic change as a struggle between words for survival:

> There was a time when out of many possible names for *father*, *mother*, *daughter*, *son*, *dog* and *cow*, *heaven* and *earth*, those which we find in all the Aryan languages were framed, and obtained a mastery *in the struggle for life* which is carried on among synonymous words as much as among plants and animals. (Müller 1862: 212)

He went on to refine this idea in his lectures:

> Hence that superabundance of synonymes in ancient dialects, and hence that *struggle for life* carried on among these words, which led to the destruction of the less strong, the less happy, the less fertile words, and ended in the triumph of *one*, as the recognized and proper name for every object in every language. On a very small scale this process of *natural selection*, or, as it would better be called, *elimination*, may still be watched even in modern languages, that is to say, even in languages so old and full of years as English and French. (Müller 1862: 383)

As Labov (2001: 14–15) notes, Darwin (see the above quotation) seeks to reduce the force of the paradox. The problem is that Spencer's metaphor of the struggle for existence, used many times by Darwin himself, does not represent an adequate statement of the process of natural selection based on variation and local adaptation. For this reason, it cannot be said that long-term functional principles determine the process of natural selection. Labov (2001: 10) quotes Greenberg in this respect:

> Taking linguistic change as a whole, there seems to be no discernible movement toward greater efficiency such as might be expected if in fact there were a continuous struggle in which superior linguistic innovations won out as a general rule. (Greenberg 1959: 69)

Labov's following comments are enlightening:

> But it is not merely the absence of evidence for evolutionary adaptation that runs counter to Darwin's argument for natural selection.

> The almost universal view of linguists is the reverse: that the major agent of linguistic change – sound change – is actually maladaptive, in that it leads to the loss of the information that the original forms were designed to carry. (Labov 2001: 10)

If we indeed believe that a Darwinian approach consists in viewing evolution as a competitive process in which the more adapted and perfect individuals survive, this criticism may make sense. But in fact such a view has nothing to do with actual evolutionary theory. Darwinian evolution, rather, has to do with variation and local adaptation through natural selection and does not concern in any fundamental way 'the survival of the fittest', that familiar slogan of the popular version of Darwinian evolution. In Chapter 3 we will return to this in more detail, and will see by means of an example why this point of view is not in fact tenable for languages.

The view that we adopt in this book, whereby languages (I-languages and populations of I-languages) are considered as CASs, is not only compatible with the contemporary view of evolution as applied to these entities, but it also offers a better understanding of natural language variation and change. CASs are indeed characterized by variation, complex interaction between their different inner components, and adaptation to their environment, resulting in the observable stability and dynamism of natural languages.

1.4 Dante's panther and Gell-Mann's jaguar

As noted in section 1.1 above, Dante used the panther metaphor as a means of visualizing the pursuit of a genuine cultivated language: a language of excellence and perfection. Many centuries later, Gell-Mann uses the jaguar metaphor in order to express the perfection that complex adaptive systems can obtain through their natural dynamics. For both Dante and Gell-Mann these felines are difficult to find and extremely elusive:

> I have never really seen a jaguar in the wild. In the course of many long walks through the forests of tropical America and many boat trips on Central and South American rivers, I never experienced that heart-stopping moment when the powerful spotted cat comes into full view. Several friends have told me, though, that meeting a jaguar can change one's way of looking at the world. (Gell-Mann 1994: 3)

The two animals pursued by these authors are intimately related to each other. The jaguar is a big cat, a feline in the *Panthera* genus, and is the only *Panthera* species found in the Americas. *Panthera* is a genus of the *Felidae* (cats) family, which includes four well-known living species: tiger, lion, jaguar and leopard. The word *panther*, while technically referring to all members of the genus, is commonly used to specifically designate the black leopard. Both the panther and the jaguar, as we have noted, are difficult to spot and to pursue, being shy and very agile animals.

Following these metaphors, we will discuss in this essay two different although closely related linguistic *beasts*: natural languages (NLs) and cultivated languages (CLs). These are difficult to pinpoint precisely, since they are both visible and invisible, objective and subjective, social and individual, mental and physical, natural and artificial. They closely resemble each other whilst being ostensibly different. Indeed, they are very similar to each other but are not the same thing, and in this essay we will try to disentangle and differentiate them.

A *cultivated language* can be characterized as a coherent series of linguistic products obtained by producing, in an intentional and purposive way, certain linguistic behaviours or phenomena, an E-Language in Chomsky's (1986) sense, during the performance of our natural linguistic knowledge, the grammatical competence that we call *natural language* (I-Language, in Chomsky's sense)

Written standard languages are a clear example of cultivated languages (CL). These languages are neither natural nor universal and develop only in certain types of human society:

> While a spoken language is found wherever human beings live together and must thus be considered part of human nature, the same cannot be said of written language, with is everywhere of much later origin and must really be called an unnatural substitute for spoken words. (Jespersen 1933: 715)

These written languages are typically established, characterized and regulated through a series of written texts. Such texts are obtained by a partially intentional elaboration of everyday or natural linguistic discourse based on the natural grammatical competence (natural language, NL) of the speakers/hearers in a particular linguistic community. For this reason, written standard languages have many grammatical characteristics of natural languages (NL) but also present many distinctive features which are either wholly or partially alien to natural language, most notably their complete uniformity, stability and lack of spontaneous acquisition. CLs do not vary spontaneously,[17] do not spontaneously change[18] and, in addition, cannot be learned spontaneously by children. They must be learned formally, most often in schools, and their rules have to be memorized and used in an intentional and controlled way. NLs are not like this. They vary, they change and they are spontaneously acquired by children; their normal everyday use does not require any specific memorization or individual or collective monitoring.

Despite these sharp differences, considerable confusion arises in the study of language, much of it arising from two main sources: a confusion of certain language products (written and oral texts and discourses) with the grammatical knowledge that makes them possible, and the confusion of CL with NL. CLs are cultural products and are the result of certain grammatical elaborations made on the products of natural grammatical competence (NL). A NL, in the sense of a grammatical competence (or of a population of grammatical competences), is a natural (not cultural) object determined by the biological principles of Universal Grammar (UG) and by the linguistic data (input) from the performance of both NLs and CLs. The conjunction of both factors makes it possible for children to build up spontaneously their own natural grammatical knowledge, the NL or I-language.

CLs correspond broadly to Dante's panther and NLs to Gell-Mann's jaguar. In the case of the animals, both are biological entities. However, whereas NLs are biologically determined natural entities in their oral (spoken languages) and gestural (signed[19] languages) manifestations, CLs are not biological, but rather cultural entities.

Notes

1. 'Sed quia unamquanque doctrinam oportet non probare, sed suum aperire subiectum, ut sciatur quid sit super quod illa versatur, dicimus, celeriter actendentes, quod vulgarem locutionem appellamus eam quam infantes adsuefiunt ab adsistentibus, cum primitus distinguere voces incipiunt; vel, quod, brevius dici potest, vulgarem locutionem aserimus, quam sine omni regula nutricem imitantes accipimus.' Translation of this and the following passages by Steven Botterill http://digilander.libero.it/letteratura_dante/translate_english/alighieri_dante_de_vulgari_eloquentia.html (retrieved in June 2011).
2. 'Cum igitur omnis nostra loquella (preter illam homini primo concreatam a Deo) sit a nostro beneplacito reparata post confusionem illam que nil fuit alliud quam prioris oblivio, et homo sit instabilissumum atque variabilissimum animal, nec durabilis nec continua esse potest, sed sicut alia que nostra sunt, puta mores et habitus, per locorum temporumque distantias variari oportet.'
3. 'Si ergo per eandem genten sermo variatur, ut dictum est, succesive per tempora, nec stare ullo modo potest, necesse est ut disiuctim abmotimque morantibus varie varietur, ceu varie variantur mores et habitus, qui nec natura nec consortio confirmantur, sed humanis beneplacitis localique congruitate nascuntur.'
4. 'Est et, inde alia locutio secundaria nobis, quam Romani gramaticam

vocaverunt. Hanc quidem secundariam Greci habent et alii, sed non omnes; ad habitum vero huius pauci perveniunt, quia non nisi per spatium temporis et studii assiduitatem regulamur et doctrinamur in illa.

4. 'Harum quoque duarum nobilior est vulgaris: tum quia prima fuit humano generi usitata, tum quia totus orbis ipsa perfruitur, licet in diversas prolationes et vocabula sit divisa, tum quia naturalis est nobis, cum illa potius artificialis existat.'
5. 'Hinc moti sunt inventores gramatice facultatis; que quidem gramatica nichil aliud est queam quedam inalterabilis locutionis idemptitas diversis temporibus atque locis. Hec cum de comuni consensu multarum gentium fuerit regulata, nulli singulari arbitrio videtur obnoxia, et per consequens nec varibilis esse potest. Adinvenerunt ergo illam ne, propter variationem sermonis arbitrio singularium fluitantis, vel nullo modo vel saltem imperfecte antiquorum actingeremus auctoritates et gesta, sive illorum quos a nobis locorum divewrsitas facit esse diversos.'
6. 'Quam multis varietatibus latio dissonante vulgari, decentiorem atque illustrem Ytalie venemur loquelam. Et ut nostre venationi pervium callem habere possimus, perplexos frutices atque sentes prius eiciamus de silva.' (Dante, I, XI, 1)
7. 'Postquam venati saltus et pascua sumus Ytalie, nec pantheram quam sequimur adinvenimus, ut ipsam reperire possimus rationabilius investigemus de illa, ut solerti studio, redolentem ubique et necubi apparentem nostris penitus, irretiamus tenticulis.'
8. 'Itaque, adepti quod querebamus, dicimus illustre, cardinale, aulicum et curiale vulgare in Latio, quod omnis latie civitatis est et nullius esse videtur, et quo municipalia vulgaria omnia Latinorum mensurantur et ponderantur et comparantur.'
9. From the point of view of the Chomskyan I and E language distinction, we propose in this book that CLs are culturally elaborated versions of the external manifestation (E-Language) of natural languages (I-languages).
10. As explained in Chapter 5, the idea that signed languages are, like spoken languages, a direct manifestation of the human language faculty is one of the most significant discoveries of contemporary linguistics. This fact cannot be ignored when discussing the natural and cultural aspects of human language.
11. See section 1.3 for an explanation of this concept.
12. We will examine a case in point in Chapter 3.
13. See Rosenbach (2008), Mendívil-Giró (2009) and the papers in Eckardt Jäger and Veenstra, eds. (2008) for critical overviews of the main proposals for an evolutionary approach to language variation and change, and Chapter 3 here for a more detailed critique of some approaches.
14. On the supposed genetic nature of constraints see below section 2.3.3.
15. Corrections of children's speech made by adults do not seem to play any significant role in natural language acquisition; indeed, some of these corrections can be severely flawed, founded on an imperfect conscious knowledge of natural grammatical rules, yet seem not to impair in any decisive way

the natural and spontaneous acquisition process. Research into 'motherese' (the special ways in which parents and caretakers talk to their children in order to facilitate the acquisition process, occurring in both oral and signed languages) has shown that although the role of parental input cannot be ruled out, neither motherese nor imitation plays a significant role in a child's language development (Bathia 2007: 17).

16. Darwin refers here to C. Lyell, who, in his 1863 book *The Geological Evidences of the Antiquity of Man*, notices a parallelism between the development of species and languages. In the first edition Darwin wrote 'curiously the same'.
17. The fact that alternative standard or written language models can co-exist in a given linguistic community is not contradictory here. Since CLs are elaborations of NLs, different varieties of the same NL can be used to produce different standard versions of the same language (American/British English, American/European Spanish, for instance).
18. As noted above, once a CL is used as an everyday language it is naturalized and begins to vary and change. Some of these changes can find their way into the original CL and hence provoke changes in it, if approved by the relevant academic authorities.
19. We use *signed languages* instead of *sign languages* in keeping with Wilcox and Wilcox (2010).

2 Exploring the naturalness of natural languages

One of the most striking consequences of the emergence of evolutionary theory in the history of human science is the conception of life as a unified phenomenon. Prior to evolutionary theory, life forms, organisms, were conceived of as essentially – radically – different: they were created different, and thus they remained. Evolutionary theory, especially the Darwinian model, changed that way of seeing the natural world by postulating that all organisms had a common origin in a primordial life form, and that all of them shared an essential core of design, a view that the so-called 'Evo-Devo revolution' has emphasized in recent decades.

Although in a different sense, the development of the naturalistic conception of language has had a similar effect on the conception of the depth of language diversity, principally through the influence of Chomsky (although such a conception can be traced back at least to Schleicher). The nativist commitment of the biological approach to human language (in which language is a biological attribute of the human species) forces an essentially unitary view of natural languages. Such a view contrasts sharply with the conception of the diversity of languages that emerges from the functionalist and cognitivist traditions (for example, see Evans and Levinson 2009a for a position that is intended to be programmatic), in which each language is said to have been 'created different', a view that in this sense can be characterized as 'pre-Darwinist'.

In the present chapter we will explore the implications of this controversy, and in what sense – and to what extent – those things that we have defined as natural languages are in fact a part of Nature. Following this, in Chapter 3, we will examine the arguments of those who reject the (literally) natural character of natural languages and propose instead that natural languages are cultural and social objects, asking what consequences this view has for the present and future science of language.

2.1 I-languages as cognitive organisms

In the previous chapter we defined natural languages as populations of I-languages, and I-languages as people's language organs.[1]

It seems, then, that there is a close parallelism between life and language, a parallelism that is particularly relevant to the task of determining how human language is part of biology. Although in the following sections we will propose a clearer characterization of the nature of I-languages, we first need to analyse in more detail the correlation between language and life, between languages and natural species.

2.1.1 Comparing languages and species

Central to this comparison is that both natural species and natural languages are, arguably, groups of similar individuals. A natural species is made up of individuals (e.g. animals) similar enough to breed other individuals, which themselves are able to reproduce. An orang-utan and a human being have more in common than an orang-utan and a cow, but all three belong to different species. We know that the greater similarity between an orang-utan and a human is due to the fact that their common ancestor is far more recent (about 6 million years) than in the case of humans and cows, which goes back hundreds of millions of years.

Meanwhile, a 'linguistic species', that is, a natural language, consists of individuals (I-languages) similar enough to allow those who possess them to communicate fluently.[2] The linguistic equivalent of the natural organism (e.g. a tiger) is each person's language organ, which we can define as the state of mind (and brain) that allows us to talk to other people (the I-language). The linguistic equivalent of the natural species (e.g. *Panthera tigris*) is the grouping of such language organs based on mutual intelligibility: the language. And likewise, while Spanish and French are more alike than French and Russian, all three are different languages. We know that the greater similarity between Spanish and French is due to the fact that their common ancestor is much more recent (about 1,500 years) than the ancestor they share with Russian (about 6,000 years).

In Biology no confusion exists between the organism and the species, but in linguistics our terminology is more confusing, as indeed are the ideas on this issue. If we accept the comparison with biology outlined above, then it would seem that the word *language* appears to serve both for the equivalent of the organism and for the equivalent of the species, something that has been – and remains – a source of much controversy and serious misunderstandings in the field of language study.

As we have seen, the identification of languages with natural organisms, or with the consideration of linguistics as a natural science more generally, were not unfamiliar to nineteenth-century historical linguistics. The best known expression of this is perhaps Schleicher:

> Languages are organisms of nature; they have never been directed by the will of man; they rose, and developed themselves according to definite laws; they grew old, and died out. They, too, are subject to that series of phenomena which we embrace under the name of 'life'. The science of language is consequently a natural science; its method is generally altogether the same as that of any other natural science (Schleicher, 1863: 20-21).

Although this paragraph has subsequently been rejected and even ridiculed (see, for example, Keller 1990), in our opinion it could be considered a historical precedent for what we now call *biolinguistic* research (see Boeckx and Grohmann 2007).

An I-language is a person's language organ, his/her faculty of language. Hence there are not around 6,000 languages in the world, but billions, as many as there are people (in fact many more, given that bilingual people are in possession of more than one I-language).

The only thing that can be said to exist, from the naturalistic (biolinguistic) point of view, are those billions of I-languages. All else (varieties, dialects, languages, families, etc.) are abstractions that we make by grouping I-languages according to their resemblances or their historical origins. The same is true in the biological realm: what exist are the emerging states of matter that we call life forms, the organisms (the billions of animals, plants, fungi, etc. living on the planet), whereas varieties, species, families, kingdoms, etc. are abstractions that we make on the basis of genetic and morphological similarity and historical origins.

Thus, an I-language is a historically modified natural object. And this is exactly what natural organisms that are grouped to form natural species are: historically modified natural objects.

Darwin used the analogy between languages and species to illustrate the theory of natural evolution, using findings from contemporary historical linguistics, especially to strengthen the idea that the similarity between similar systems could be explained as an inheritance from a shared common ancestor (see Alter 1999; Mendívil-Giró 2006, 2009). As we saw in the previous chapter, Darwin identified species with languages, and organisms with the components of languages (words, sounds). Most modern versions of the analogy between languages and species are based on this type of correlation between the two orders (language = species, components of a language = organisms). This is not so in the case of Schleicher. In his review of the German version of *The Origin of Species*, he deals with the correlation as follows:

> The species of a genus are what we call the languages of a family, the races of a species are with us the dialects of a language; the sub-dialects or patois correspond with the varieties of the species, and *that which is characteristic of a person's mode of speaking* corresponds with the individual. (Schleicher, 1863: 32, our italics)

What Schleicher mentions as 'that which is characteristic of a person's mode of speaking' is the closest definition that could be formulated at the time of the concept of I-language. And, as suggested, the most appropriate terms of comparison are those that identify, on the one hand, I-languages with the organisms that form a species, and, on the other, natural languages (understood as a population of similar I-languages) with species.

But these language organs, in addition to being natural objects, are also historical objects. The language organ of a person who speaks English is different from that of a person who speaks Spanish: both share (allegedly) a fundamental design, which conventionally we call Universal Grammar (UG, see section 2.2.), but differ as a result of contingent events that can only be explained historically. Migrations, divergent changes, borrowings and isolation have produced two different natural objects (actually, millions of them, as many as there are speakers of both languages). But it is important to note that the very fact that the I-language of an English speaker and the I-language of a Spanish speaker are historically different should not make us think that they are purely historical objects, just as a horse and a buffalo are different historical objects, but are not purely historical, but also natural.

A 'linguistic species' (like a natural species) comprises a group of individuals with a requisite number of similarities. The degree of this necessary similarity is determined by viable reproduction in the case of natural species (Mayr 1942) and by mutual intelligibility in the case of languages (Dixon 1997). And in both cases it is a diffuse and somewhat arbitrary border, as we will see. In the case of species, reproductive potential depends on a very pronounced morphological and genetic similarity between two individuals; in the case of languages, mutual and fluent intelligibility depends on a very pronounced lexical, grammatical and phonological resemblance between two language organs, but also on the individual attitudes and capabilities of people.

The comparison works because (as argued by Pinker 1994, Chapter 8) the evolutionary mechanism is based on the same principles: inheritance, mutation and isolation. Heredity explains why organisms resemble their descendants (lions breed lion cubs, not chicks); mutation explains why descendants are not exactly identical to their progenitors; replication is imperfect. Genetic mutation and other factors generate variation among organisms, and it is through the variation of organisms that natural selection operates. Isolation prevents natural selection becoming homogeneous in all populations and results in the unequal distribution of variants among different populations.

The case of languages is comparable; children speak the same language as their parents (assuming that they raise them), but not exactly the same. Sometimes reanalysis (or errors) generates variation, and it is variation that feeds the social selection that leads us to adopt and transmit new forms, along with traditional ones, to successive generations. Physical and social barriers prevent the homogenization and levelling of the relative frequency of variants.

Nevertheless, many linguists do not accept this view, in the sense that they argue that *the language* (English, Spanish, Russian) is what really exists, I-languages being manifestations of these external languages in the minds of people. In contrast to the internalist approach we are advocating here, this would be an externalist approach in that it gives ontological primacy to the concept of language as a shared social or cultural object (one of the meanings of the fuzzy Chomskyan concept of E-language, coinciding with our notion of cultivated language, that is, a social projection of natural languages).

A clear instance of such an externalist approach is that of Terrence Deacon:

> In some ways it is helpful to imagine language as an independent life form that colonizes and parasitizes human brains, using them to reproduce. (Deacon 1997: 111)

This is a fascinating point of view, but entails significant difficulties, perhaps the most pressing being that of the very nature of the object under study. In this and other externalist theories (to be discussed in Chapter 3), there is a tendency to believe that the real object of study is not I-language (that is, a person's language organ) but rather an external language; that is, language as a shared social object.

It is implied, then, that external languages are what really exist, whilst I-languages are nothing but manifestations or reflections of these entities in individual minds. This is essentially Saussure's (1916) notion of *langue*, which is of course widely extended among philosophers of language:

> Si nous pouvions embrasser la somme des images verbales emmagasinées chez tous les individus, nous toucherions le lien social qui constitue la langue. C'est un trésor déposé par la pratique de la parole dans les sujets appartenant à une même communauté, un système grammatical existant virtuellement dans chaque cerveau, ou plus exactement dans les cerveaux d'un ensemble d'individus; car la langue n'est complète dans aucun, elle n'existe parfaitement que dans la masse. (Saussure 1916: 30)

Notwithstanding the popularity of this position, it is in fact rather a strange stance from a naturalistic point of view, and is more or less comparable to the idea that what really exists is the species (e.g., the species of horses, *Equus ferus*) and that the individuals (horses) are nothing but manifestations of this species.

It seems more reasonable to say that what really exist as natural objects are horses and individual I-languages, and that natural species and natural languages are nothing but populations of those objects. Clearly, the social dimension of language does exist, but it is not part of natural language, but of cultivated languages.

So, we have now established how such terms can be properly used. If we are asked how many languages exist in the world, our response ought to be that 'it depends'. If I-languages, then there are billions; if natural languages, then perhaps a few thousand (between five and seven thousand being the figure most often given in textbooks and encyclopaedias). If we are asked what is a language, then, we must also replay that 'it depends'. If I-languages, we can say, vaguely, that an I-language is a person's system of knowledge, a cognitive organism, a state of his/her mind/brain; if asked about a natural language, then we must say that it is a set of I-languages bearing a suitable similarity to each other.

2.1.2 Delimiting natural languages

Such an answer, albeit the best we can give at this stage, raises many problems. One of these is what counts as *suitable similarity*, that is, the degree to which similarity is required in order that two I-languages can be said to belong to the same natural language.

Not surprisingly, the same problem arises in biology. How do we know if any two organisms belong to the same or to different species? How do we decide if two organisms that are very similar, but which have some differences, are two varieties of the same species or belong to two different species? The traditional and intuitive criterion is that of fertile breeding. Although it is a somewhat simplified approach, species are often defined as reproductive communities (Mayr 1942). Thus, a mastiff and a chihuahua are relatively different animals, but we group them in the same species (*Canis lupus*) because, at least in theory, they can breed other dogs, which in turn can continue to do so. A buffalo and a bull are relatively similar animals, but belong to different species (*Syncerus caffer* and *Bos taurus*) because they cannot breed. Far from being an objective and clear criterion, fertile reproductive capacity is a relatively arbitrary and fuzzy criterion. What about donkeys and horses? While officially they belong to two different species (*Equus ferus* and *Equus africanus*), they may procreate with each other. Since the offspring from crosses of donkeys and horses (mules) are usually infertile, we decide that they belong to distinct species.

The criterion for defining the limits of a natural species, then, is diffuse and relatively arbitrary, and the same applies to languages. Indeed, the issue is somewhat aggravated here by the relatively inaccessible and abstract nature of linguistic individuals, that is, of I-languages. Linguists can only investigate the nature and structure of I-languages by analysing the linguistic behaviour of people, looking at the utterances they produce, those ones they do not produce, and the differences between these in different human groups.

The history of linguistics as a science is an uninterrupted attempt to build theoretical models of these systems of knowledge we call I-languages, and which are presented to us as being grouped or fragmented into natural languages, and which in turn give rise to cultivated languages. Linguistic research has provided a great deal of information on the internal architecture of these systems, on their interaction with other cognitive and cultural systems, and on the degree to which they are similar or different; all these answers, nevertheless, remain partial and tentative.

Many researchers (including quite a few linguists) believe that such a relatively deep knowledge of the structure and properties of languages can be useful when determining whether any two I-languages are examples of the same language or are from two different ones. But this is not in fact the case. The problem here has nothing to do with the degree of our knowledge of the structure of languages, but with another false belief: the belief that natural languages and E-languages have an independent existence beyond those I-languages that we find within people. It seems as if given two specific examples of I-languages, our task should be to decide whether they belong to one or another natural language.

Indeed, we often do this, but in appearance only: in fact what we do is try to determine (based on similarities and differences) what kinds of I-languages are more similar to these productions. Note that it is not a matter of identity or membership in a mathematical sense, but of a greater or lesser degree of similarity. If we hear an extract of recorded speech and we are asked to determine if the voice is talking, for example, in Spanish or in Italian, in a way we try to determine to which group (Spanish or Italian) this production *belongs*; however, what we actually do, be us accomplished Romanists or amateurs, is to assess which of the two groups of known I-languages (what we call Spanish and Italian) has more similarities with the extract in question. Such a task would typically present us with few problems, but what is significant is that there is in fact no objective criterion or procedure for making the decision.

It will always be an arbitrary criterion based on the fuzzy notion of *sufficient degree of similarity*.

If we are presented with an extract that is a mixture of the two languages, our decision is likely to be arbitrary. In essence (although to a different degree) that's what happens whenever we decide that a particular linguistic expression belongs to this or that language.

Since our decision is usually based on the degree of similarity, the crucial issue, then, is how we determine what degree of similarity qualifies as sufficient, that is, how we determine in what ways and to what extent two I-languages should resemble each other for us to consider them variants of the same natural language. While this issue is often frustrating for the uninitiated, the only scientific answer that linguistics can offer is that the criterion should be one of mutual intelligibility, and that if given any two I-languages their users should be able to understand each other.[3]

The problem, though, is that mutual intelligibility is also a matter of degree; yet we have to impose at some point an arbitrary criterion for deciding whether or not there is mutual intelligibility. This is so because, as noted in the previous chapter, I-languages are not tokens of previously defined types. Many people think that I-languages are like mathematical objects (note here the false belief that E-languages exist as independent objects) so that given several examples, we can determine objectively their typological identity. If we are given any set of natural numbers (for example 3, 5, 34, 35, 45, 64 and 83) we can state without a doubt which ones belong to the sets of even and odd numbers, and which are prime numbers. Crucially, this operation is not based on estimates of degree of similarity: no number exists which is more even than 34 but less odd than 35.

Suppose that instead of a set of numbers we are given a set of animals (e.g. two mice, a rat, and a cat) and we are asked to classify them by species. Obviously we cannot provide a mathematical demonstration of which class they belong to, nor can we *demonstrate* that the two mice belong to the same species. The best we can do is to compare them gene by gene. If we do so, at some point we would be in a position to say that the two mice share more genes with each other than with the rest of the organisms, and based on this we could decide that they belong to the same species, excluding the other animals. Of course, we would be right, not as in the case of numbers, but simply because we have established that the degree of similarity between the two mice is high enough as for grouping them, arbitrarily, into the same class. Note that although we claim that the criterion is arbitrary, this does not mean it is an irrelevant criterion; it simply means that we have previously established, based on criteria external to the object itself, the limit that we consider sufficient. In this sense, the task of deciding whether two I-languages belong to the same natural language is more like classifying animals than numbers.

All of this leads us to conclude that the underlying reality is a continuity. Despite appearances, this is what is real, both in biology and in linguistics. We have seen that the so-called biological concept of species (Mayr 1942) is not without its problems. In general it is a clear criterion that focuses on reproductive isolation, but that does not mean it is mathematical and exempt from fuzziness. Thus we have the well known case of so-called ring species. A ring species is a connected series of neighbouring populations, each of which can mate with the adjacent one. However, so many differences have accumulated between distant populations within the ring that these can no longer interbreed. Some gene flow between populations is still possible, however, across the 'fertile borders'. When such populations, which are genetically connected but cannot mix with each other, live in close proximity, they are said to be a ring. The best known case is that of certain arctic gulls (*Larus*). The problem, of course, has to do with the biological fact that fertile reproduction is not a transitive relation. If A can interbreed with B we say that A and B are part of the same species. If B can interbreed with C we say that B and C are part of the same species. Yet A and C, which cannot interbreed, must then be both the same and different species. Ring species show that the biological concept of species is not as clear and robust as in principle it appears to be.

This should come as no surprise to linguists. Dialectal continua were described early in the nineteenth century, and Bloomfield (1933) defined them as dialectal areas whose ends lost inter-comprehension:

> The difference from place to place is small, but, as one travels in any one direction, the differences accumulate, until speakers, say from opposite ends of the country, cannot understand each other, although there is not a sharp line of linguistic demarcation between the places where they live. (Bloomfield 1933: 51)

Does all this mean that natural languages, understood as populations of I-languages, do not exist at a certain level or are irrelevant? Certainly not! Such an assertion would be like claiming that the fact that natural organisms are grouped into species is irrelevant or secondary from the point of view of biological research. Clearly, with respect both to organisms and to I-languages, the arbitrary clusters we make between them are relevant to explain their natures, but this should not distract us from the reality of the underlying continuity that they represent as real phenomena.

2.1.3 I-language vs. E-language

Since we have defined a natural language as a population of I-languages, both notions can be considered related to the natural or biological dimension of language, and therefore independent of the social and cultural (i.e. collective) dimensions of human languages. Following Chomsky's terminology, we call E-language the social and cultural projection of human languages.

The term E-language has many uses in the literature (see for example Chomsky 1986; Smith 1999; Isac and Reiss 2008), and some of these uses are indeed striking if we recall that in originally coining the term Chomsky intended it to be unconnected to what we now call biolinguistics:

> The notion of E-language has no place in this picture. There is no issue of correctness with regard to E-languages, however characterized, because E-languages are mere artifacts. We can define 'E-language' in one way or another or not at all, since the concept appears to play no role in the theory of language. (Chomsky 1986: 26).

In general, generative linguistics sees E-language as a heterogeneous and inconsistent object, since it is defined either as the set of utterances produced by a community, as the result of language use, or as a social or cultural institution.[4] Indeed, such notions are irrelevant to the 'biolinguistic' point of view, which of course does not imply that they are also irrelevant for other, perfectly licit, approaches.

Thus, we do not intend to question the idea that human languages have a relevant social and cultural dimension worthy of study in itself. What we intend to question is that this is the true nature of so-called natural languages, as well as to point out how inconsistent it is for linguistic theory to give ontological preference to E-language over I-language, which more or less explicitly characterizes at least part of current linguistic theory.

In fact, it could be said that conferring ontological primacy on E-language over I-language is what really differentiates the two major linguistic paradigms that have existed over the last 50 or 60 years, what for convenience we might term the *biolinguistic paradigm* (including Generative Grammar and any other naturalistic approach to language) and the *functional-cognitive paradigm* (including an extensive list of functionalist traditions and authors, many of which have recently moved towards so-called cognitive linguistics).

If we begin with E-language as the basic object, considering *à la* Saussure that I-languages are manifestations of E-languages in the minds of speakers, then an anti-naturalistic conception of language emerges, a conception in which natural languages are conceived of as cultural, and not as natural objects. Such a conception is the common basis of the functional-cognitive paradigm (FCP) and the cause, as we shall see, of two of its main features: an exaggerated assessment of the depth of the diversity of languages, and the rejection of the notion of a human faculty for language.

If we overlook the naturalistic point of view and take as our point of departure the upper level (that is, E-language), our conclusions about the nature of human language will end up hopelessly distorted, since E-languages (groupings of similar I-languages) are themselves defined using a differential criterion with other E-languages. To put it another way: if we lose sight of this continuous grid which underlies our higher order differential groupings (groups of similar I-languages), we will fail to see that all I-languages are in fact different developments of the same object, the human faculty of language.

If, on the contrary, our main ontological commitment is to the I-language (although for practical reasons we talk about natural languages), then we will be better able to temper the obvious diversity that change over time creates in clusters of I-languages, and we will also be in a better position to approach the study of human language as a property of the species, the only legitimate scientific goal from a biolinguistic point of view. That is, if we base our approach on this continuous network of I-languages, we will be better able to explore the startling claim made by Chomsky (1995: 7) that, outside surface variation, all humans speak the same language.

As we have suggested, if one adopts a biolinguistic point of view, the relationship between language and languages is proportional to the relationship between life and life forms, organisms. Of course, what we find in the physical world are organisms and not life itself. Life exists only as life forms, and it is quite true that these are notoriously diverse. But this is not to deny that life exists (that is, in contrast to the inorganic world), or that we should consider it a secondary matter to ask which common properties define and explain it. Indeed, this is the central goal of biology as a science.

There is no reason to believe that this shouldn't also be the case in a biolinguistic approach, unless we reject the comparison, thus rejecting the notion that all existing languages are manifestations of the same faculty of language, and instead sustain the view that languages are essentially cultural objects, abstract tools that have evolved independently and whose essential structure comes from outside the human mind and brain.

As we hope to show, it is precisely this conception of language and languages, an anti-biolinguistic (i.e. anti-naturalistic and externalist) conception that characterizes the research programme of the FCP, and which feeds what we might refer to as the myth of the diversity of languages.[5]

2.2 Diversity in nature and in language

2.2.1 The myth of language diversity

That languages are different is an objective fact, not a myth. What we call *the myth of language diversity* is the belief that the diversity of languages is profound and sufficiently substantive to be considered the crucial phenomenon in the scientific study of language.

Indeed, the comparison between I-languages and natural organisms could be used as part of an anti-universalist position in justification of the depth of the diversity of languages, in the sense that there is a noticeable difference in the structure and way of life between (at one end) a bacterium and (at the other) a human being, with its brain composed of some hundred billion (10^{11}) neurons. And because of this we believe the comparison is legitimate, in that the diversity among languages is as remarkable and significant for the study of language as the diversity of species is for the study of life. The way in which languages differ is, then, an excellent source of information on how the brain constructs, processes and uses language.

It is noteworthy that from a phenotypic point of view life forms are extremely varied, but it is also true that all forms of life use the same chemical processes and biological mechanisms to develop, metabolize, reproduce and die. Compared to inorganic objects, forms of life are fundamentally similar. In fact, biochemist Michael Sherman (2007) has suggested that given an abstract enough perspective, there would be only a multicellular organism with surface patterns of variation, which is clearly reminiscent of Chomsky's statement mentioned above.[6]

To dismiss or underestimate the biological and natural foundation of language would be comparable to renouncing the discovery of the basic principles of life in favour of a descriptive analysis of living forms and of the induction of certain patterns or processes common to all of them. Nobody, of course, proposes this in the sphere of life sciences, but in language science this is indeed the case.

Many readers will have noticed the implied reference in the title of this subsection to the influential paper by Evans and Levinson (2009a): *The Myth of Language Universals*. Evans and Levinson do indeed believe that Universal Grammar (UG) is a myth that Chomskyan linguists have injected into cognitive science, something that constitutes an obstacle to the scientific investigation of language: 'a great deal of theoretical work within the cognitive sciences thus risks being vitiated' (Evans and Levinson 2009a: 429).

Evans and Levinson react against Chomskyan universalism arguing that it distorts the reality of language, compromising realistic and meaningful research within cognitive science:

> The claims of Universal Grammar, we argue here, are either empirically false, unfalsifiable, or misleading in that they refer to tendencies rather than strict universals. Structural differences should instead be accepted for what they are, and integrated into a new approach to language and cognition that places diversity at centre stage. (Evans and Levinson 2009a: 429)

However, it could be said, on the contrary, that it is the exaggerated assessment of the depth of the diversity of languages which constitutes an obstacle to the ultimate acceptance of the study of language as one of the natural sciences. Disdain of the diversity of languages can certainly be an obstacle to progress in our understanding of how the brain creates and uses language. But what Evans and Levinson propose, in their rejection of universality, ignores important discoveries about common properties of language made over the past half century and risks throwing the baby out with the bath water.

Evans and Levinson explicitly formulate this 'myth' as one of their conclusions:

> The diversity of language is, from a biological point of view, its most remarkable property – there is no other animal whose communication system varies both in form and content. (2009a: 446)

While it is undeniable that the diversity of human languages is notable and relevant, the claim that diversity is the most remarkable property from the *biological standpoint* can indeed be challenged. Their statement appears to be based on the belief that no other animal communication system varies in form and content as much as human language does. However, this is doubly questionable. First, Evans and Levinson's assumptions as to the degree of variation in the form and content of human languages is not in itself beyond dispute. Second, it is not clear whether indeed no variation exists in other animal communication systems.[7] For example, many songbirds have dialectal variation:

> Most birds do not simply mimic the song of adults exactly: In many species, individuals create new, novel songs that are built upon but not identical to the songs they heard as nestlings. This creative aspect of birdsong ensures that each generation hears slightly different songs from those of the previous generation. This process of song transmission across generations, with slight novelties introduced by creativity and or erroneous copying, leads to 'dialects' of birdsong: Birds in different regions sing quite different learned songs. (Fitch 2009: 289)

It is difficult to consider this description without reflecting on what happens in the case of human languages, unless we apply different criteria to humans than to other species. 'Language' change and diversification, then, is not so rare in the natural world. However, naturalists have not been tempted to conclude from this that there are organisms of the same species that have radical and profoundly different systems of communication and knowledge, except in the case of humans (as can be seen in the quotation from Evans and Levinson, above).

It is tempting to consider this as an example of the kind of suspension of scientific rationality in the studying the human being that Chomsky has frequently noted when defending the naturalistic approach to human language.[8] What Chomskyan naturalism means in this sense is that the burden of proof is on those who deny that human beings have a unique capacity for language and who claim that this ability varies greatly and deeply across the species. Certainly this would be a strange biological fact, unless of course we think that language has nothing to do with biology and nature.

The radical and deep diversity of languages is in this sense a myth, a myth built on the old anthropocentric belief that humanity can be seen as essentially a matter of culture rather than nature, and that human languages are cultural artefacts, not natural objects.

2.2.2 The myth of human nature as culture

The frequent insistence on the plasticity of human cognition and on the power of our ability to learn cannot be interpreted other than as an attempt to present human language as a phenomenon alien to the natural world:

> Structural diversity at every level is not consonant with a theory of fixed innate language structure, but instead suggests remarkable cognitive plasticity and powerful learning mechanisms. We pointed out that human communication is the *only* animal communication system that varies in myriad ways in both form and meaning across the species, and this must be a central fact that should never be lost sight of. (Evans and Levinson 2009b: 473)

Faced with a similar criticism of dualism by Smolensky and Dupoux, Evans and Levinson claim:

> Smolensky and Dupoux ignore the recent synthesis of biological and cultural evolution. Thus they assert 'language is more a biological than a cultural construct.' We would go further: 'language is one hundred percent a biological phenomenon.' (Evans and Levinson 2009b: 479)

The *number one enemy* of the FCP is the assumption that human beings have a natural capacity for language (that which has traditionally been called UG). Yet, as we will discuss in greater detail below, this is a false problem, and mainly a terminological one. The attack on UG simply disguises an assault on the consideration of human language as a natural object and, ultimately, on the idea that the human mind is also a natural object.

One possible explanation as to why a non-naturalistic conception of human beings is linked to the rejection of a naturally conditioned faculty of language (FL) would be that if we recognize the existence of such a capacity as a component of the human mind, what follows is the idea that the other components of the mind would be similar or largely identical to those of other organisms, something that collides with the anthropocentric idea that there are substantial differences between humans and other animals. As Penn *et al.* point out:

> At present, most comparative psychologists believe that the difference between human and other animal minds is 'one of degree and not of kind' (Darwin [...]). Among researchers willing to admit that the human mind might be qualitatively different, most argue that our species' cognitive uniqueness is limited to certain domain-specific faculties, such as language and/or social-communicative intelligence. We believe this view of the human mind is profoundly mistaken. In our opinion, the discontinuity between extant human and nonhuman minds is much broader and deeper than most researchers admit. We are happy to report that Evans and Levinson's target article strongly corroborates our unpopular hypothesis. (Penn *et al.* 2009: 463)

As we know, the hypothesis of a natural capacity for language is the Chomskyan answer to the 'spectacular fact (...) that any normal human child can learn any human language, and no human language is learnable by any other extant species' (Penn *et al.* 2009: 463). As these authors ask, 'why are human languages so easy for us to learn and so unthinkable for everyone else?' (*ibid.*), Chomsky's response that only humans are endowed with a human FL as part of their nature 'fits nicely with the presumption that the rest of the human mind is more or less like that of any other ape' (Penn *et al.* 2009: 463). One way to reject such a conclusion, undesirable from an anthropocentric point of view, is to support the myth of the diversity of languages:

> But as [Evans and Levinson] point out, the diversity of human languages suggests that our faculty for language relies largely on domain-general cognitive systems that originally evolved for other purposes and still perform these non-linguistic functions to

> this day. If [Evans and Levinson] are right, there should be significant differences between human and nonhuman minds outside of language. (Penn *et al.* 2009: 463)

Evans and Levinson themselves point out, as a remarkable fact about our species, that the same set of organs (the same in all people) serve in the acquisition and use of a set of heterogeneous and radically different languages (2009b: 479). In fact, this is a serious problem for the contention that languages are radically diverse. To adopt Chomsky's own phrase, this would be more a mystery than a problem. But we can try to make it a problem by using the logic of rational inquiry, which by default supposes that behind similar but apparently diverse and heterogeneous systems (be they physical phenomena as in the behaviour of fluids, natural organisms or human languages) there underlies a set of principles and parameters of variation that can reveal the root causes of similarities and, of course, of differences.

2.3 The Human Faculty of Language and the nature of Universal Grammar

2.3.1 Innatism and emergentism

The functional-cognitive model runs counter to Chomsky's postulation of a specifically linguistic and specifically human Faculty of Language (FL), and argues that it is more economical, more biologically plausible, and more consistent with standard scientific reasoning to assume that no such thing exists, and that languages can be explained as the result of general limitations of learnability, the recruitment of other cognitive systems, and functional pressures arising from their use for communication and thought. This is certainly a possibility, one which the minimalist program developed by Chomsky and followers has in fact been exploring over the last 15 years (see section 2.4).

It could be said, then, that what has confronted the different traditions in linguistic research over the last 50 years is the problem of the innate or emergent character of the FL. However, this is a false problem, a false controversy, because FL, like any other human faculty, is simultaneously innate and emergent. On the one hand, there is no doubt that human beings have an ability that enables them to learn and use any human language. Given that the rest of known organisms (whether natural or artificial) lack such an ability, it is fair to say that this ability is specifically human and, therefore, innate in any normal human being. As Chomsky points out:

> to say that 'language is not innate' is to say that there is no difference between my granddaughter, a rock and a rabbit. In other words, if you take a rock, a rabbit and my granddaughter and put them in a community where people are talking English, they're all learn English. (2000: 50)

Fitch follows this same elementary line of reasoning:

> Clearly, immersion in a linguistic *environment* is not enough for spoken language to develop in most organisms. There must therefore be *something* about human children which differentiates them from other species, and this something provides one of our core *explananda* in biolinguistics. We might gloss this neutrally as 'the human capacity to acquire language'. In generative linguistics this capacity is traditionally called the 'Language Acquisition Device', and a characterization of its properties termed 'Universal Grammar'. (Fitch 2009: 288)[9]

On the other hand, it cannot be false to claim that human language (as a human ability) is emerging, that is, the result of the combination or the arrangement of elements that in themselves are not language. To return to our analogy between life and language, life is certainly an emergent phenomenon, but by no means less real because of this. As Stuart Kauffman puts it:

> life is not located in the property of any single molecule – in the details – but is a collective property of systems of interacting molecules. Life, in this view, emerged whole, [...], not to be located in its parts, but in the collective emergent properties of the whole they create [...] The collective system is alive. Its parts are just chemicals. (Kauffman 1993: 18, 24)

In fact, Chomsky himself, when describing FL as a subcomponent of the brain that is specifically dedicated to language, notes: 'As a system, that is; its elements might be recruited from, or used to, other functions' (Chomsky 2004: 124, fn 1).

Rothstein and Treves (2010) note that 'evidence accumulated over the past century, but little noticed by linguists, indicates that there is no dedicated neuronal machinery to subserve complex cognitive capacities, least of all machinery specialized for language' (Rothstein and Treves 2010: 2717). In this sense, it seems that 'our abilities to learn, produce and interpret language are supported by the same neural mechanisms, at the cortical micro-circuitry level, as any other cognitive function, including those (most) that we share with other mammals' (*ibid.*). Nevertheless, they add that 'while something is known about the neural mechanisms underlying, for example, visual and auditory processes, we know next to nothing about how the nervous system processes information about the relation between sounds and symbols and how complex meanings are represented compositionally in the brain' (*ibid.*). Although we can infer that cortical transactions behave in the same way in language as in other, better understood functions, 'how they sum up to produce the faculty of language, and why they should do so only in the human species, remains unclear' (*ibid.*).

The solution proposed to address this mystery is simply to accept that language, as an emergent system, may have its own properties, so that linguistic structures themselves will be the result of a particular organization and accumulation of neural processes that are necessarily (and inevitably) more basic:

> The mystery may stem precisely from the nature of language as an emergent property, its being more than the sum of its parts, arising, that is, by the system-level combination of elementary cortical operations. From such a perspective, the central question for cognitive neuroscientists is what neural mechanisms can facilitate compositional interactions, and how the range of grammatical structures emerges from a much narrower range of neural mechanisms. Further, what is the nature of the plasticity which allows children to acquire a native-speaker linguistic competence in a finite time; that is, how do children learn to manipulate a finite set of symbols in such way that they can produce and interpret an infinite number of novel strings and thus convey and comprehend new information. (Rothstein and Treves 2010: 2717–2718)

A similar view is that of Marcus (2006), who suggests that the possible mental organization of cognitive (or functional) modules can be relatively independent of the modular organization of the brain in neurobiological terms, while the possible neurobiological modules may themselves be relatively independent of genetic modules.

Of course, much research remains to be done to determine the shape, nature, extent and evolution of the principles governing the origin, development and use of the language faculty, but it makes no sense to focus the controversy *a priori* in terms of ideas about the false issue of innateness and emergence of FL.

If we define UG as the initial state of FL (the human capacity to learn language in Fitch's terms), that is, as the set of natural principles (whether genetic or not, whether biological or not) that determine the architecture of human languages and limit their ranges of variation, UG by definition exists. Of course, it could be argued that the very definition of UG, which claims that these principles are specifically linguistic (in fact, specifically grammatical, if we stick to the literal interpretation of the term) is the problem. This is Tomasello's objection:

> For sure, all of the world's languages have things in common, and Evans and Levinson document a number of them. But these commonalities come not from any universal grammar, but rather from universal aspects of human cognition, social interaction, and information processing – most of which were in existence in humans before anything like modern languages arose. (Tomasello 2009: 471)

Two separate issues underlie such an objection: a question of terminology, and the suggestion that languages arose subsequent to the human empowerment for language. The first issue will be discussed in the remainder of this chapter, and the second will be dealt with in the following chapter.

2.3.2 Why not Universal Grammar?

The terminological problem clearly has to do with the meaning of the expression *Universal Grammar.*[10] Note that Tomasello does not reject the possibility that language universals exist, but only that the properties that explain them are specifically linguistic:

> Why don't we just call this universal grammar? The reason is because historically, universal grammar referred to specific linguistic content, not general cognitive principles, and so it would be a misuse of the term. It is not the idea of universals of language that is dead, but rather, it is the idea that there is a biological adaptation with specific linguistic content that is dead. (Tomasello 2009: 471)

But we can ask what is meant by 'a biological adaptation with specific linguistic content'. Does it mean that there would be genes that specify grammatical categories? Or that there would be parts of the brain dedicated to language and whose removal would leave intact all non-linguistic cognitive and motor faculties? Or that there would be linguistic neurons and non-linguistic neurons, just as there are pyramidal and spherical neurons? No one seems to have defended such a position. The idea of a 'biological adaptation with specific linguistic content' is in fact a straw man. Innatism refers to the bias that the body and the laws of nature underlying the body's anatomy and physiology impose on the systems of knowledge that are developed. If everyone agrees that this bias exists, then the dispute is meaningless.

Most certainly, UG is a heterogeneous set, since it may include restrictions derived from the principles that govern brain development and even purely formal principles that apply to every system of memory and computation. The notion of UG, which for historical reasons alludes to grammar, does not in fact presuppose that each and every one of the principles that form it have to be specifically linguistic.

The question as to which of the principles governing the formation of LF in each person are specifically human and specifically linguistic (if any) is an empirical matter, and it cannot be resolved prior to the determination of what such principles are. The distinction between the Faculty of Language in a narrow sense (FLN) and in the broad sense (FLB) of Hauser *et al.* (2002), and the factorialization formulated by Chomsky (2005) (which is common in developmental biology) are simply attempts to make this more explicit in the investigation of FL (see 2.3.3. below).

Evans and Levinson concede that this is more of a terminological than a real problem, and suggest talking about the human capacity for language, avoiding the term UG:

> To make this crystal clear: UG/FLB must include all the infrastructure for language including the neuroanatomy for speech and cognition, theory of mind, statistical learning capacities, and all the communicative and cooperative motivations and interactional abilities special to the species (...). If all this is agreed, it is time to change the terminology and avoid all the theory-laden terms used so far. We would urge our colleagues simply to talk about *the human capacity for language* (including language-special aspects of cognition, if any) and the ingredients or elements that may contribute to that – the rest carries too much baggage, as the field advances rapidly beyond the creaky old baggage train. (Evans and Levinson 2010: 2742, our italics)

However, the question is not whether linguistic principles and structures may be reduced to more basic principles and structures (and ultimately to neuronal structures and developmental processes), but when, how and at what level the reduction can be done without ceasing to account for the structure of languages.

2.3.3 The rise of minimalism: Towards biological adequacy

Given the orderly and structured appearance of living beings, and given the need to eliminate the action of a creator as the ultimate explanation, it was thought that the primary source of such order may lay in the adaptation to environment through natural selection. This proposal, Darwin's, is clearly important and following the development of genetics came to be associated with a geneticist conception of the development of organisms, a vision in which the environment itself is of scant import during development and the process is entirely governed by the genetic programme. Such was the prevailing view in biology during the 1950s and 1960s, precisely when generative grammar emerged (Chomsky 1955/1975), and remains largely so today, even if things are changing very quickly in biology.

The geneticist model of development was especially attractive to the Chomskyan (naturalist and internalist) approach to human language, in that it addressed a similar problem: how to explain the robustness and consistency of human language development in an unstable and confusing environment which provides very poor evidence on the systems of knowledge finally obtained. Consequently, the initial models of Chomskyan generative grammar, culminating in the *Principles and Parameters* model (Chomsky 1981; Chomsky and Lasnik 1993), focused on an innate, rich and specifically human linguistic component as an explanation of the so-called Plato's Problem.

Of course, Chomskyan linguistics was not aimed at the study of the possible 'language genes', but focused on opposing the view in the science of language that language development is a process based on imitation, induction and generalization performed by general systems of learning. If the Chomskyan model was essentially geneticist until the years 1980–1990, then, it was simply because it was a naturalistic model, a model which argued that language is a natural phenomenon common to our species, and that linguistics should be understood as part of biology, the science that studies the form and structure of organic beings. Since the prevailing biology was geneticist, generative grammar was geneticist by simple inheritance. Looking back at the literature of the time we find statements by Chomsky and other distinguished generativists attributing Universal Grammar to the human genome,[11] but not because they attribute certain properties of UG to certain genes (an absurd claim for those working with syntactic categories and agreement features rather than with proteins and codons), but because it was assumed that what is naturally specified, what is 'innate' or not learned, corresponded to what is genetically specified.[12]

Although geneticism in developmental biology continues to prevail, things have changed a great deal in recent decades, and so-called Evo-Devo models (from 'evolutionary developmental biology') have transformed current evolutionary biology into a much more pluralistic field of research. In short, the new evolutionary biology has shown that the neo-Darwinist radical alternative 'or God or natural selection' was too restrictive in the sense that neither a creator nor natural selection are sufficient in themselves to explain the structure and evolution of life. As Stuart Kauffmann pointed out, 'biology since Darwin is unthinkable without selection, but may yet have universal laws' (Kauffman 1993: 25).

Longa and Lorenzo (2012) note that the neo-Darwinian model, gene-centric and based on the notion of a genetic programme (which the authors call 'preformationist'), has been questioned in recent decades by the so-called 'developmentalist challenge'. The gene-centred model implies that genes are the only possessors of the essential information that guides the growth and maturation of organic structures. Genes are considered, then, to be a stand-alone programme that includes information on the patterns of structural organization and the instructions for the deployment of these structures in time and space. This view can be considered 'preformationist' because it implies that the sources of organic development are already contained in the information in the nuclear DNA and that the process of development will be the eclosion of what is already contained in the genes.

According to the new biology of development (which focuses more on epigenesis) phenotypic traits (whether anatomical, physiological or cognitive) cannot be contained or specified in genes. This implies that the notion of 'genetic programme' as the only source of information for developmental processes is a distorted vision of how such processes occur, as it ignores the significant contribution of other factors and resources located between genotype and phenotype without which the development process simply cannot occur.

On the contrary, the model that focuses on development (commonly referred to as DST, 'developmental system theory', see Benítez-Burraco and Longa (2010) and references therein) suggests breaking the identification between form and genetic coding and rejecting the conception of the genome as the only source of organic form and as the only (or even the main) causal agent of development. DST is a theoretical approach to development, heredity and evolution which downplays the importance of genes to the extent that it rejects the existence of a genetic programme, instead favouring of a view of genes as one of many available resources for developmental processes. The crucial notion in the DST model is 'development system', to be understood as a set of different influences on development, of which genes are just one element.

Geneticism and adaptationism have been closely related in evolutionary biology, and indeed the new evolutionary biology is neither adaptationist nor geneticist. As previously pointed out, generative grammar has been geneticist as a consequence of its environmental heritage and as a counterpoint to empiricist and behavioural theories of mind and language, but it has never been adaptationist. A solid illustration of this is Daniel Dennett's treatment of Chomsky in his influential book on the internal logic of the neo-Darwinian model (Dennett 1995). Dennett links Chomsky and Stephen J. Gould[13] in a kind of vicious circle of loyalties with the ultimate goal of rejecting the (supposedly) 'Darwin's Dangerous Idea':

> In short, although Gould has heralded Chomsky's theory of universal grammar as a bulwark against an adaptationist explanation of language, and Chomsky has in return endorsed Gould's anti-adaptationism as an authoritative excuse for rejecting the obvious obligation to pursue an evolutionary explanation of the innate establishment of universal grammar, these two authorities are supporting each other over an abyss. (Dennett 1995: 391)

Dennett accuses Chomsky of being a 'skyhook seeker' not because he believes that Chomsky is a creationist, but because of his known resistance (e.g. Chomsky 1988) to accept adaptive explanations of the evolution of the language faculty:

> But although Chomsky uncovered for us the abstract structure of language, the crane that is most responsible for lifting all the other cranes of culture into place, he has vigorously discouraged us from treating it as a crane. No wonder yearners for skyhooks have often taken him as their authority. (Dennett 1995: 397)

Even as Dennett published his influential book, Chomsky (1995) was developing the so-called Minimalist Program (MP), a research programme specifically aimed at trying to clarify which aspects of the Faculty of Language are a consequence of the biological endowment of the species (which can therefore have evolved adaptively and can be genetically encoded) and which are due to principles of simplicity, computational elegance, or brain developmental processes, factors which, therefore, are not the result of evolutionary adaptation but rather a consequence of the evolution of the human brain or a result of deeper formal or physical principles governing systems of a certain complexity.

In fact Chomsky (2005) notes that a key issue to solve from the point of view of the biological study of language is the extent to which the principles that determine human language are unique to this cognitive system or whether similar formal arrangements can be found in other human cognitive domains or in other organisms; yet 'an even more basic question from the biological point of view is how much of language can be given a principled explanation, whether or not homologous elements can be found in other domains or organisms' (2005: 1). And this is precisely the goal of MP, to look for a 'principled' explanation of the principles attributed to UG.

As Chomsky (2007) noted more graphically, MP consists in approaching the content of UG from below and not from above:

> At the time, it seemed that FL must be rich, highly structured, and substantially unique. [...] Throughout the modern history of generative grammar, the problem of determining the character of FL has been approached 'from top down': How much must be attributed to UG to account for language acquisition? The MP seeks to approach the problem 'from bottom up': How little can be attributed to UG while still accounting for the variety of I-languages attained? (Chomsky 2007: 2, 4)

Though not always explicitly recognized (although see Boeckx 2012 and Longa and Lorenzo 2012 for recent exceptions), such a minimalist approach necessarily involves embracing some of the arguments long advocated by those who, over the last thirty or forty years, have opposed the Chomskyan innatist and modularist conception of language. This is certainly good news for the future of linguistic science, though at this point we probably lack the required historical perspective to make a definitive statement as to the real contribution of recent schools of linguistic thought to the linguistics of the future.

This space of reconciliation offered by MP (even if only collaterally) has not prevented the two great 'paradigms' of language research continuing to make very different assessments of issues such as the degree of the diversity of languages, the reasons for and directions of language change, or indeed the very conception of the nature of language and languages. According to the orientation which guides us in the current book, this is a consequence of an inadequate (or in some cases nonexistent) delimitation between the natural and social dimensions of human language.

In the following section we will consider which concept of natural language (I-language) emerges from a minimalist approach to the biology of human language, and in subsequent chapters we will return to the controversy discussed above.

2.4 The minimalist anatomy of I-languages

2.4.1 Components and factors of language design

A direct consequence of the minimalist approach is the acceptance of the need to decompose the object of study (the Faculty of Language) to try to determine which of its components are specifically human and which are not, and also which are the result of natural selection and which are not.

This is the main objective of the influential formulation of Hauser *et al.* (2002), in which a distinction is established between the faculty of language in a narrow sense (FLN) and in the broad sense (FLB). This latter includes all of the different mechanisms implied in the knowledge and use of language, regardless of their overlap with other cognitive domains or even with other species. Essentially, Hauser, Chomsky and Fitch propose that FLB includes a sensory-motor system (SM), a conceptual-intentional (CI) system, other possible systems, and the computational mechanisms for recursion ('Narrow Syntax').[14]

Given that language as a whole is specific to human beings, it is plausible that a set of FLB is uniquely human and language-specific. This set is what Hauser, Chomsky and Fitch call FLN:

> FLN is composed of those components of the overall faculty of language (FLB) that are both unique to humans and unique to or clearly specialized for language. (Fitch *et al.* 2005: 182)

Importantly, they note that the contents of FLN must be empirically determined and, of course, that it could be an empty set. In such a case (i.e. if it were proven that no component of FLN is uniquely human and specifically linguistic), then we would conclude that the only thing that is specifically human is the particular arrangement of these components in our species.

They hypothesize that FLN 'comprises only the core computational mechanisms of recursion as they appear in narrow syntax and the mapping to the interfaces' (Hauser *et al.* 2002: 1573); more explicitly they assert that:

> A key component of FLN is a computational system (narrow syntax) that generates internal representations and maps them into the sensory-motor interface by the phonological system, and into the conceptual-intentional interface by the (formal) semantic system. (Hauser *et al.* 2002: 1571)

One of the main advantages of this model is that it is compatible with the hypothesis that FLB is a species adaptation that shares many aspects with other species' systems of knowledge and communication while maintaining simultaneously that the mechanisms underlying FLN are specifically human and specifically linguistic.

We already know that the crucial question for the minimalist programme is 'how little can be attributed to UG while still accounting for the variety of I-languages attained' (Chomsky 2007: 7). Chomsky's formulation of this new question takes its most radical form (known as the Strong Minimalist Thesis, SMT) thus: to what extent is FLN designed in a 'perfect' way to satisfy the requirements imposed by the cognitive systems (internal and external to FL) with which it interacts?

By 'perfect' design Chomsky meant the ideal case in which the computational system would have a minimal design, that is, a design made only of the properties indispensable for the system to be usable, hence accessible by the systems with which it interacts. In Uriagereka's words:

> given the contingent fact that language is used, which yields some conditions that are external to the system, is there a perfect (if you will), conceptually necessary, and optimally economic way of meeting those external conditions? (Uriagereka 1998: 77)

The minimalist inquiry falls within the context of modern biology (and of science in general) in which the key challenge is to explain extremely complex systems from simple principles, and in which the appeal to the genome as the 'development program' simply does not serve as an explanation.

A key step in this direction is the decomposition of the various factors involved in the development of such systems. Since an I-language is a cognitive organism, Chomsky (2005) suggests applying to the study of I-language development the same factorization that is usual in the investigation of other organisms:

> Assuming that the faculty of language has the general properties of other biological systems, we should, therefore, be seeking three factors that enter into the growth of language in the individual. (Chomsky 2005: 6)

He characterizes these three factors as follows:

> Factor 1.
> Genetic endowment, apparently near uniform for the species, which interprets part of the environment as linguistic experience [...], and determines the general course of the development of the language faculty. (Chomsky 2005: 6)

> Factor 2.
> Experience, which leads to variation, within a fairly narrow range, as in the case of other subsystems of the human capacity and the organism generally. (Chomsky 2005: 6)

> Factor 3.
> Principles not specific to the faculty of language. The third factor falls into several subtypes: (I) principles of data analysis that might be used in language acquisition and other domains; (II) principles of structural architecture and developmental constraints that enter into canalization, organic form, and action over a wide range, including principles of efficient computation, which would

> be expected to be of particular significance for computational systems such as language. It is the second of these subcategories that should be of particular significance in determining the nature of attainable languages. (Chomsky 2005: 6)

Chomsky (2007, fn. 6) adds to the factors of the third type those properties of the human brain that determine which cognitive systems can exist. This shows that the notion of 'third factor' is deliberately inconsistent. 'Third factor' is a term intended to encompass any relevant aspect in language development and structure which is not language specific.

Arguably, in terms of these three types of factors, the Principles and Parameters (P&P) model relied more on type 1 factors and the MP model on type 3 factors. In other words, the P&P model endorsed a more geneticist 'environment' of the biology of the time (the years 1970–1990), while MP echoes the developmental biology revived in more recent times, and thus constitutes a serious attempt to integrate linguistics and biology into the study of human language, and a definite route for the possible integration of diverse (and frequently contradictory) approaches to language.

As already mentioned, the strategy developed in minimalist research is to build the theory 'from the bottom up', that is, assuming that the principles governing the construction of language knowledge are general, and considering the factor 1 (UG) as the residue of what is non-attributable to type 3 factors, then:

> UG is what remains when the gap has been reduced to the minimum, when all third factor effects have been identified. UG consists of the mechanisms specific to FL, arising somehow in the course of evolution of language. (Chomsky 2007: 5)

2.4.2 The basic elements of human syntax

The minimalist idea that UG is biologically simple and minimal should not be construed as an assertion that human language or languages are themselves simple. This, of course, is in no way the case. The ability to build sophisticated and complex thoughts and to transform them unconsciously and automatically into sounds or visual signals through a motor system, and to intentionally use them to mean any number of things, real or unreal, past or future, involves a varied and intricately woven assembly of cognitive and neurological systems that even now we are only beginning to understand.

When it is asserted that UG (and in particular FLN) is biologically minimal, what is being claimed is that the biological differences, especially genetic ones, between the evolutionary stages just before and after its emergence in our species were minimal, which also implies that this process was probably a relatively brief and sudden event, not a gradual and lengthy process of evolution over time, on a geologic scale.

One way to make coherent the biologically minimal nature of UG with the resulting complexity of the 'phenotype' (the I-languages people speak, not to mention languages as social and cultural objects, E-languages) is, as noted, the decomposition of FL in various components that may have an independent evolutionary history and a diverse nature.[15] Thus, the key to the 'discontinuity' that seems to exist between human language and other species' systems of communication and cognition (including other forms of human communication) would not be the unlikely biological evolution of a complex organ, which would not have had time to evolve (especially given that no trace of it is found in other, closely related species), but rather a biologically minimal event that furnished the complex pre-existing systems with the 'extra ingredient', resulting in new and unexpected properties.

The SMT posits precisely this: that the FLN would include only what is necessary so that the linking of a conceptual system and a motor/perceptual system could produce a system of knowledge with the properties which characterize human language. Continuing the well known development of his ideas on the evolution of language, Chomsky (2007) explicitly raised the hypothesis that what made language emerge in our species was just a small change associated with the crucial ingredient of FLN: the operation *unbounded merge*:

> At the minimum, some rewiring of the brain, presumably a small mutation or a by-product of some other change, provided Merge and undeletable EF [edge features] (unbounded Merge), yielding an infinite range of expressions constituted of LIs [lexical items] (perhaps already available in part at least as conceptual atoms of CI systems), and permitting explosive growth of the capacities of thought, previously restricted to the elementary schemata but now open to elaboration without bounds. (Chomsky 2007: 14)

Note that what Chomsky proposes is that the 'syntactic machine' provided by unbounded merge, that is, the ability to join two units recursively, is essentially a 'language of thought', that is, an ability to link together concepts in a new and unlimited way:

> Such change takes place in an individual, not a group. The individual so endowed would have the ability to think, plan, interpret, and so on in new ways, yielding selectional advantages transmitted to offspring, taking over the small breeding group from which we are, it seems, all descended. (Chomsky 2007: 14)

This scenario suggests that the computational system that is FLN (which produces the 'internal syntax' to which we refer below in more detail) was initially considered, and indeed would remain to be considered, a 'language of thought' independent of communication and of the externalization systems: 'the earliest stage of language would have been just that: a language of thought, used internally' (Chomsky 2007: 13).[16]

This view crucially implies that the relationship between FLN and the CI and SM systems is asymmetric. Chomsky (2007 and later) argues that there are clear indications that the design of FLN, the internal syntax, is optimized for its connection and interaction with the CI system, and not for its connection and interaction with the SM system. This asymmetry would explain why it is in the process of 'externalization' (and 'materialization') of the internal syntax where linguistic diversity appears:

> Various considerations, then, seem to converge rather plausibly on the conclusion that language may be optimized relative to the CI interface, with mapping to SM an ancillary procedure, and complex to the extent that SM has no prior adaptation to these needs. Insofar as SMT holds, generation of structures mapped to CI will be optimal for the CI interface and common to languages apart from parametric and lexical choices (phenomena that require explanation), while phonology, morphology, and whatever else is involved in externalization might be variable and complex and subject to large-scale historical accident, satisfying the linking condition in ways that are as good as possible. (Chomsky 2007: 14–15)

According to this model, the internal syntax would be minimal (in the sense that it would be governed by criteria of computational efficiency), universal (common to all languages) and invariant (insensitive to historical change); syntax would be a computational system to generate concepts from concepts. The 'externalization' of the internal syntax (which would result in the I-languages spoken by people) would imply that the internal syntax is linked to systems external to the FLN (but internal to the FLB, which we call SM for short) including what is commonly known as morphology and phonology (i.e., an 'internal lexicon' in a sense to be specified below), in addition to other sensory-motor systems that lead to the effective materialization (in sounds or visual signs) of syntactic derivations.

Evidently there is an apparent contradiction in the statement that the internal syntax is *externalized* in a given *internal* language (I-language). Here we must note that an I-language is a mental organ, a system of knowledge (hence the 'i'), which includes a biologically determined component (internal syntax) but also a component 'internalized' from the environment, which is precisely what distinguishes the world's languages from each other.

As Sigurdhsson (2011) has pointed out, albeit using different terminology, we must distinguish between the emergence of the internal syntax, a biologically determined process during brain development, and the subsequent (though early) processes of development of the (internal) lexicon and morphology, a process strongly influenced by the environment and helped by general learning resources (one of the subcategories of the type 3 factors mentioned by Chomsky):

> That is, early internal language growth is 'nativistic'. In contrast, lexical and structural expansion in later learning of external language, including second language learning, evidently involves internalization. (Sigurdhsson 2011: 374, n. 14)

An I-language thus includes an I-syntax, and a morphology and a phonology 'internalized' from environmental stimuli (factor 2). This then implies that the SM component that is part of the FLB is much more complex and structured than it would be if it only included the already complex systems involved in the production (and interpretation) of sounds or visual signs. In this sense, we might say that the morphology and phonology of a language (what we call the I-lexicon specific to each language) is a component developed in the process of language acquisition which is external to the FLN but internal to the FLB; in other words, it is the interface between FLN and the SM system.

According to the anti-symmetry hypothesis of Berwick and Chomsky (2011), the incorporation of the SM component of the FLB is 'ancillary' or secondary to the relationship between CI and FLN, to the extent that Berwick and Chomsky suggest that SM would not even have evolved for language (in fact, in terms of evolution it is much older than other components of FLB). This would explain why I-languages change and diversify, and above all, why language does not appear to be optimized for communication, but for thought, which falls squarely within the traditional controversy between formalists and functionalists in relation to language functions and its adaptation to them (see Newmeyer 1998).

The following quote from Chomsky, neatly and informally summarizes this point of view and sets it in relation to learning and language change:

> But what about the relation between this internal system and the sensory motor system? That's the externalization problem. Well, the sensory motor system had been around for hundreds of thousands of years. It's a completely separate system. It has nothing to do with this internal entity. So there is a hard problem to solve. How do I relate that internal system to the sensory motor system for externalization? Well, it's a hard problem and in fact if you look

> at language, that's where practically all the complexity of language is. When you study a second language, about all you study is externalization. You study the sounds, the particular lexical choices, which are arbitrary, the inflectional system, you know, how to conjugate verbs, some facts about word order, and so on. That's just about all you have to learn. You don't have to learn the syntax and the semantics because that's there already. That's part of your nature and probably it's part of your nature because that's the way physical laws work. It's meeting conditions of computational efficiency – or so we would like to show. The externalization systems are overwhelmingly – maybe, some day, we will discover entirely – where languages differ from one another. The wide variety of languages is almost entirely, maybe entirely if we know enough, in the externalization process, the secondary process of getting it out into the sensory motor system. That's also where languages are very susceptible to change, so say teenage jargon or invasion or something else. That's where languages change a lot. That's where they vary. (Chomsky 2010a: 20–21)

The crucial idea is that the interfaces between this internal universal syntax and the rest of the components of language (broadly defined) are different for each human being, because they are sensitive to external experience during their development (the type 2 factor), and therefore they are grouped culturally. But note that if we were to claim that languages are essentially different, then we would be identifying 'language' with the historically modified interfaces, that is, we would be excluding from the definition of language that which (hypothetically) is common to them all, hence making the claim that they differ sharply a trivial one.

If we substitute for the question *how deep is the diversity of languages?* the question *how deep is the diversity among species?* it is easier to perceive that there is no clear and objective answer. If one focuses on the external phenotype (e.g. body size or nervous system) the difference between an orang-utan and an earthworm is enormous. If we continue down to the embryonic level, similarities increase and differences decrease; at the genetic level the degree of similarity is even greater, and if we move into the biochemical mechanisms that drive cells, we reach indistinguishability. If we really are to take seriously the naturalistic approach, the same logic should be applied to languages.

It is quite possible that the human genome specifies very little about what is a possible human language, but it is also true that the genome specifies little about what is a possible human pancreas. In spite of this, each human will develop a pancreas essentially homogeneous in the species, because the development of this organ (and that of all the others), in addition to being genetically bound, is strictly constrained by epigenetic and environmental factors and, of course, by principles of development, biochemistry and physical laws. The language organ does not escape this logic, although among the 'environmental' factors there is, plausibly, a far greater variety (see Longobardi 2003). However, when biologists talk about the influence of the environment on the developmental process, they are referring principally to the environment of the cell, not to the environment of the organism, which has an undeniable influence, but a far more mediated one. The same applies to language. The environmental (non-genetic) factors that regulate language development are also (but not exclusively) internal to the brain and internal to the language faculty, in a broad sense. It is precisely here, with these factors, that we should look for language universals (and probably for typological tendencies), and not in the ultimately derived languages, that is, in the different patterns of externalization.

As we have seen, Evans and Levinson propose as an alternative research programme to the biolinguistic one, a model in which 'the natural' is first separated from 'the cultural', and in this way it can be denied (rightly) that there are exceptionless universal properties in the phenotypic realization of languages. Evans and Levinson accuse some of their critics of using a definitional notion of UG, rendering it unfalsifiable (Evans and Levinson 2010: 2741), but they in fact do the same, but in the opposite direction: they consider a priori that human languages are cultural systems, thus excluding from the very concept of language the natural conditions that it can have, given that in their model such conditioning is by definition language external. Therefore, the notion of language with which they operate is partial, the result of segregating biological invariants (factors 1 and 3) from what is subject to historical development. It is hardly surprising, then, that they fail in their attempt to find linguistic universals.

Returning to our analogy between language and life, we might say that Evans and Levinson do not find the common basis of life, because they do not look for it in biochemistry, in the principles of self-organization, in the laws of development or in epigenesis, but rather in genes and phenotypes, where they cannot exist, since this is the domain of the contingent historical events that have singled out each species (and each language).

In a way, we can say that the model suggested by Evans and Levinson to address the problem of the uniqueness and diversity of languages is an incomplete one that reproduces the same limitations that characterize the neo-Darwinist model of natural evolution. Neo-Darwinist biologists tend to downplay the sources of order and structure of organisms other than adaptation by means of natural selection. And in the same vein, functional-cognitive linguists tends to downplay the principles that determine the uniformity of languages, and to identify as the sources of the observed uniformity those principles derived from the functions (adaptations) for which language is used.

As we have suggested, the functionalist idea that language can be explained as the result of adaptation to aspects external to language itself (see, e.g. Givón 2009: 336–337) has an undeniable similarity to the strong minimalist thesis (SMT) and, in fact, it can be said that the MP provides a good opportunity to reconcile those traditions into the study of language that have been in conflict for centuries.[17]

Yet there is a significant difference that we should not overlook. When in the functionalist tradition language is explained as the result of external functional constraints, it conceives of language as a communication system and, therefore, the external sources of structure adduced as factors in the development of language and languages have to do with language real-time use and processing in communicative acts (see, for example, Hawkins 2004). However, as we have seen, from the point of view of the MP, the relevant 'third factor' in explaining the development of FLN has nothing to do with communicative efficiency, but with computational efficiency. The fact that many syntactic properties of languages follow from principles of simplicity and computational economy in the derivation is actually an argument in favour of the view that the internal syntax is not a communication system, but a computational system linked, perhaps isomorphically (see Pietroski 2011), to the CI component, with its relation to SM component being secondary or ancillary.

What this means, on Berwick and Chomsky's (2011) view, is that 'externalization', which obviously serves communication, is not a simple task: it has to relate two different systems, the SM system (which quite plausibly has been the same for hundreds of thousands of years) and the computational system that (supposedly) singles out our species. Accordingly, morphology and phonology, the processes that make syntactic derivations accessible to the SM system, should be intricate, varied and certainly sensitive to historical change:

> Parameterization and diversity, then, would be mostly – possibly entirely – restricted to externalization. That is pretty much what we seem to find: a computational system efficiently generating expressions interpretable at the semantic/pragmatic interface, with diversity resulting from complex and highly varied modes of externalization, which, furthermore, are readily susceptible to historical change. (Berwick and Chomsky, 2011: 37–38)

If so, it would be wrong to place communicative functionality as the essential basis of the explanation of linguistic structure, just as it would be a mistake to seek the explanation of the nature and structure of the human hand in its use for typing, however widely and effectively we use the hand in this sense. Nevertheless, it makes sense to look for this kind of pressure or effect in the process of language externalization itself and in its use for communication, something that opens up a wide range of possible intersections between both stances, and allows us to conclude that minimalist research, while maintaining a formal and internalist approach to language, promotes the integration of those external functional pressures that have always captivated functionalist linguists.

Notes

1. According to Chomsky, 'The I-language is, then, some element of the mind of the person who knows the language, acquired by the learner, and used by the speaker-hearer' (Chomsky 1986: 22).
2. Of course, we speak of 'linguistic species' only in a comparative sense, without implying that humans have more than one kind of natural language per se. On the contrary, we believe that all humans share a common faculty of language (see discussion in section 5.2).
3. This is the approach that Dixon (1997) calls linguistic criterion. All the other criteria we use are (also in terms of Dixon) political criteria. So, to give relatively clear examples, according to linguistic criteria Serbian and Croatian are the same language, but according to political criteria they are two different languages. Not many years ago, Serbo-Croatian was considered a single language from a political point of view, which highlights the linguistic arbitrariness of such a criterion.
4. As Smith points out, 'While it is usual to talk of "the English language" as spoken in different continents and in different centuries, there could be no mental or psychological reality to an entity so dispersed in space and time. The popular use is convenient, but disguises the fact that language in this sense does not correspond to a scientific domain. Crucially, there are no laws or principles that hold of "English", "Chinese" or "Dutch" as social or national constructs, any more than there are principles that hold of the Dutch visual system; but there are (grammatical) principles that hold of the linguistic knowledge of each individual' (Smith 1999: 151).
5. See Mendívil-Giró (2012), on which we will elaborate in the next section.
6. Reminiscent of Chomky's approach is the notion of *Universal Genome* used by Sherman.
7. On the other hand, that languages are used for communication does not mean that they *are* systems of communication. In fact, it is highly questionable that communication is a unitary biological organ or system susceptible of evolution (see discussion in Lorenzo 2012).
8. 'The basic properties of humans seem to be identical, close to identical, except

for pathology, which you can find anywhere. So you could investigate every individual, just like you could investigate every apple to make sure it follows the laws of motion when it falls, but nobody does that because there is so much evidence that they have to be identical. In fact it's interesting that these questions only arise in the human sciences. They never arise in physical sciences. It's all the same. Why don't they arise elsewhere? Because there is a kind of rationality that prevails in the study of the natural world, which is somehow cancelled when we study ourselves. At that point we become very irrational. So we ask the kinds of question that wouldn't arise in studying other aspects of the physical world – even studying other animals.' (Chomsky 2010a: 30).

9. As Rooryck *et al.* point out, 'As human language differs from all other systems something (but not necessarily some thing) must be unique' (Rooryck *et al.* 2010: 2655).
10. Chomsky (1966) took the expression from rationalist philosophers and grammarians who opposed universal grammar to particular grammar to refer to those aspects which as were assumed common to all languages should not be reported – in fact, were not recorded – in particular grammars. Thus, it was important to say in a French grammar that there are articles, but not, for example, that in French there are words and phrases.
11. See Benítez-Burraco and Longa (2010: 314, fn.9) for some examples.
12. As Uriagereka points out, 'UG isn't about genes, but about formal properties of human language. UG could equally be true if human beings were made from musical notes instead of genes' (1998: 47).
13. Gould is the most renowned anti-neo-Darwinist, who Dennett repeatedly accuses of trying to replace the 'cranes' with 'skyhooks'. In Dennett's terminology, a skyhook (in front of a crane) is a concession to creationism, a rejection that neo-Darwinism is the only possible explanation of life and its structure.
14. They point out that FLB 'excludes other organism internal systems that are necessary but not sufficient for language (e.g., memory, respiration, digestion, circulation, etc.) (Hauser *et al.* 2002: 1571).
15. The basic problem of developmental biology is to explain the conversion of genotype on phenotype. One way to facilitate this explanation is obviously to simplify the phenotype, and that is the goal, in the field of language development, of the MP.
16. See Hinzen (2011) for a defence of the hypothesis that the internal syntax is the same as the 'language of thought' and for arguments against proposals that seek to distinguish between them.
17. If only because functionalists and cognitivists have always rejected the notion of a biological adaptation for language (see Tomasello 2009), which is precisely what the SMT aims to minimize.

3 The paradox of languages without a Faculty of Language

It is clear that human languages are cultural objects as well as tools used by people for various social and cognitive purposes. We do not intend to challenge this, but to note that conceiving of languages exclusively in these terms is empirically inappropriate and causes an erroneous bias in the assessment of the degree of diversity of languages, and also an inadequate conception of language change and of the evolution of the faculty of language in our species.

In our view, much of the misunderstanding in this regard come from an inadequate identification between the cultural and the historical dimensions of human languages, in the sense that it seems to be argued that if languages are historical objects then they must be cultural objects and not natural ones. We believe that this conclusion is false. Once we separate the biological and cultural aspects of human language we find that the historical dimension is not peculiar to one dimension (the cultural one) but is relevant to both domains. For this reason we have been inspired by the example of natural evolution in that natural organisms, like I-languages, are simultaneously natural and historical.

3.1 Languages as cultural objects

Insofar as languages are cognitive organs, their variation is limited by the biological conditioning that restricts human nature, just as organisms are restricted in their variation by the range of production of proteins made available by chemical properties of DNA. To the extent that languages are historical objects, they show variation as a result of their peculiar and contingent history, and in the same way living organisms show variation as a result of their peculiar and contingent evolutionary history.

Even more importantly, the analogy proposed here might permit us to conclude that if organisms are really historical variations on the same theme, languages are too. Although we believe that this is a perfectly legitimate inference, it is also true that it cannot be made directly. The crucial issue, it seems to us, is that in the domains of both evolutionary theory and linguistic change, there is no general agreement regarding the extent of the 'creative' capacity of evolutionary processes like natural evolution or linguistic change.

When we define a language as a historically modified mental organ, we are assuming that linguistic change is the main cause of linguistic diversity, a conclusion identical to Darwin's when he suggested that organisms' mutability explained the existence of different species. Therefore, the question of the extent of linguistic diversity approximates to a very great extent to the question of the transforming capacity of the change process in languages. Can processes of linguistic change produce anything that is not a language? The answer seems clear: no. On the other hand, can linguistic change produce a language from anything that is not a language? Again, the answer seems to be *no*. And although current theoretical approaches have not wholly reached a consensus on this, it is the answer we are going to follow here.

In fact, many authors think that linguistic changes were a central part of the evolution of language (e.g., Givón 2009; Heine and Kuteva 2007). This conclusion, we think, owes a lot to an inadequate conception of language and of evolutionary theory. If, for the moment, we restrict ourselves to evolutionary theory, we must recall that two principal schools or traditions exist, the neo-Darwinist tradition and what we will call anti-neo-Darwinist.[1]

The main difference between the two approaches is related to the role of natural selection and the adaptive character of evolutionary changes. Neo-Darwinists assume that every feature of an organism is the outcome of an adaptation process that occurs by means of natural selection. Anti-neo-Darwinists, in turn, stress that adaptation cannot explain all existing morphology and insist on the contribution of laws of form and other principles that canalize or restrict the structure of organisms.

Gould (2002) has explained the terms involved using the metaphor of Galton's polyhedron, taken from Darwin's 'brilliant and eccentric' cousin Francis Galton. According to a neo-Darwinist point of view, an organism can be conceived of as a moving billiard ball. When the cue hits the ball, it produces different and variable ball movement. Unrestricted variability exists. The cue is natural selection and the ball goes wherever 'selection' pushes it. According to Gould, this conforms to an externalist, functionalist, and adaptationist theory of evolution. In contrast, from an anti-neo-Darwinist point of view, the organism would be like a polyhedron that remains positioned on one side unless it is pushed hard enough so that it topples onto an adjacent side. Of course, the action of natural selection is necessary, but once the polyhedron is hit, the possibility of change is internally constrained. The polyhedron has a structure that restricts variation in such a way that some options are more probable than others and certain options are impossible, regardless of how interesting they might be adaptively.

Thus, whereas Gould and numerous others do not deny natural selection and its importance as a mechanism, they claim that we must also make a thorough study of the influence of negative restrictions (and/or positive channels) on Darwinian adaptations. What is at issue is in fact not whether Darwin was right, but whether he was absolutely right, that is, if the distribution of the morphology and structure of life forms is simply the result of adaptation through natural selection, or whether other factors that place limits or somehow channel the evident work of natural selection are also in operation. As Kauffman suggests, the matter is that 'we do not understand the sources of order on which natural selection was privileged to work' (Kauffman 1993: 643).

The main difference between the two viewpoints, then, lies in the degree of relevance conceded to physical laws and to auto-organization principles in explaining the existing morphology. For a neo-Darwinist, the limits are so lax that all existing morphology follows from natural selection, whereas for an anti-neo-Darwinist, the 'skewed occupancy of morphospace' (in Gould's terms) is the outcome of certain restrictions, and the evident labour of natural selection is not enough to explain the forms attested. In simpler terms, the neo-Darwinist model focuses more on differences, while the anti-neo-Darwinist one focuses on resemblances and on possible restrictions on variation.

This is a familiar controversy in linguistics. It is a subject of debate in the literature on linguistic diversity, as these two well known but contrasting quotations illustrate:

> Languages can differ from each other without limit and in unpredictable ways. (Joos 1957: 96)

> There is only a computational system and one lexicon, apart from its limited kind of variety. (Chomsky 1995: 170)

It could be said that for Joos languages are historically like billiard balls, while for Chomsky they are like polyhedrons. Although not specifically an argument in this debate, it is important to note that modern evolutionary biology tends to encourage the pluralistic view of evolution rather than that brought about by the neo-Darwinist synthesis:

> Pluralism, instead of the belief in the omnipotence of natural selection, is the norm in evolutionary biology today. [...] Obviously, natural selection only serves as a filtering condition on preexisting variations, and the primary question is how these variations first came into existence. In other words, arrival of the fittest, instead of survival of the fittest, is the core issue in any evolutionary study. (Narita and Fujita 2010: 364)

Notice how remarkable the parallelism with linguistics is in this context. Neo-Darwinists deny the existence of 'laws of form' or other factors that restrict or channel the work of natural selection further than fundamental physical laws, and functional linguists do not accept the existence of specifically linguistic principles or mental structures that restrict the ways in which languages can change beyond what is learnable or usable in general.

What this implies is that we are confronting non-internalist approaches to language. However, if a language is not a natural object, then it must be a purely cultural object. Martin Joos' position might seem old-fashioned, but in fact quite the contrary is true. It is, more or less explicitly, the stance that functional and cognitive linguistics has taken during the last 30 years, and is clearly adopted by Haspelmath (2008) and by Evans and Levinson (2009a).

In our opinion, what these traditions share is that they are functionalist (externalist) approaches to both language and the mind. What is essential to a functionalist approach is what is of relevance: not an object itself, its inherent structure, but rather what it is used for or what functions it has. Focusing on human language, one can say that for the formalist, language is an attribute of the human mind/brain, whereas for the functionalist, language will be *represented* in the mind/brain. However, if it is represented, then it is external to the mind and the brain.

This predicts a scenario in which linguistic changes are restricted only by the functions that must be met for communication and thought, which in turn would imply that languages can diverge freely provided that the functions entrusted to them are met. Thus, from the externalist, functionalist and adaptationist view (to use Gould's characterization), a language is by definition a historical object that has been created as a result of its development through successive adaptive changes.

On the contrary, from an internalist, formalist and non-adaptationist viewpoint, a language is, of course, a historical object (affected by the Basque substrate, the Norman conquest, etc.), but it is also a natural object with an 'ahistorical' structure which marks boundaries, the pathways opened or closed to changes. This model predicts that linguistic changes are superficial, and therefore also predicts a restricted range of language diversity.

Given that for functionalists languages are essentially cultural historical objects, the patterns of similarity among languages must be explained either by shared historical heredity, or by evolutionary selective pressures *external* to the evolving systems:

> To the extent that there are striking similarities across languages, they have their origin in two sources: historical common origin or mutual influence, on the one hand, and on the other, from convergent selective pressures on what systems can evolve. The relevant

> selectors are the brain and speech apparatus, functional and cognitive constraints on communication systems, including conceptual constraints on the semantics, and internal organizational properties of viable semiotic systems. (Evans and Levinson 2009a: 446)

Note that in the absence of further specification, this statement cannot be false. This amounts to saying that the explanation of the structure of organic beings must be the result of natural selection, the laws of self-organization of organic matter, developmental principles and physical laws. The central issue, in both biology and linguistics, is to define what degree of restriction changes present, be they evolutionary (in the case of natural organisms) or historical (in the case of languages).

As regards evolutionary biology, Gould makes the central question clear:

> In what ways does the skewed and partial occupancy of the attainable morphospace of adaptive design record the operation of internal constraints (both negative limitations and positive channels), and not only the simple failure of unlimited number of unconstrained lineages to reach all possible position in the allotted time? (Gould 2002: 1053)

Gould argues strongly in favour of the first option, on the basis, among other arguments, of the discovery in modern genetics of a deep homology between taxonomical types separated by more than 600 million years. These types share many ontogenetic channels based on levels of genetic retention (e.g. the so-called Hox genes) that a neo-Darwinian model would consider implausible, given the alleged capability of natural selection to modify any line in a single direction according to its long and contingent history.[2]

Not surprisingly, Evans and Levinson (2009b) argue to the claim of Pinker and Jackendoff (2009) that languages actually occupy the space of conceivable design very much to a partial extent, that such a partial occupation could be a consequence of the fact that languages have not yet had time to develop in certain ways, given the short span of their evolution (about 100,000 years, according to Evans and Levinson).[3] It is impossible to judge this argument, since there is no way of knowing objectively whether 100,000 years is a long or short period of time in this sense. It is, though, instructive to see how Evans and Levinson, perhaps inadvertently, align themselves conceptually with the neo-Darwinian point of view, according to which the evolutionary process is limited externally and not internally to the evolving system itself.

In fact, the neo-Darwinian idea that the methodology of evolutionary theory can be applied wherever any dynamic system exhibits random variation, selection between variants, and differential inheritance, is probably correct, and as we have shown is clearly applicable to languages. Yet this does not mean that there is only one way of conceiving of the methodology of evolutionary theory, or that there is only one way to think of languages as dynamic systems with random variation and differential inheritance.

In the tradition represented by Deacon (1997) and Hurford (2002),[4] to which Evans and Levinson's (2009a) programmatic article is definitely indebted, when they speak of a language as a dynamic system they are actually talking about E-language, while I-language is a mere reflection of the former in the brains/minds of speakers, who merely transmit it with changes.

Although in some ways the analogy is appropriate, in the sense that language change occurs through iterated learning processes, the problem is that the object of study is located *outside* speakers. E-language is identified with the species, but there is no clear equivalent of the natural organism, the individual forming the species.

A conclusion shared by those working in this tradition share (Briscoe 2002: 10) is that languages evolve by adapting to acquisition requirements, a surprising way of seeing the issue which again illustrates that we are operating with a biologically inconsistent notion of language, as E-language, an external object, or as a set of sentences. This approach may sound appealing, but in the end it is unacceptable, since it would be analogous to claiming that natural organisms have evolved to be expressed by DNA. Obviously, DNA is not part of the environment to which organisms adapt, and in the same way acquisition requirements imposed by human brains are not part of the environment to which languages adapt, unless we claim that languages are objects outside the brain and not properties/states of the brain itself. Indeed, such is the case with Deacon's influential theory of brain and language co-evolution:

> The extra support for language learning is vested neither in the brain of the child nor in the brains of parents or teachers, but outside brains, in language itself. (Deacon 1997: 105)[5]

Let us imagine a stone channel through which water circulates. Of course we can say that water is adapted to the shape of the channel, but it would be surprising if we were to ignore the fact that the channel structure also strictly determines the form water adopts. Notice that the problem is not whether learnability requirements are general or are specifically linguistic (a difficult and central issue, but ultimately an empirical one), but one of considering them part of the adaptive environment for languages. And this is indeed the usual point of view of the FCP:

> Human children appear preadapted to guess the rules of syntax correctly, precisely because languages evolve so as to embody in their syntax the most frequently guessed patterns. The brain has

> co-evolved with respect to language, but languages have done the most of the adapting. (Deacon 1997: 122)

For this externalist and adaptationist conception, in which languages evolve independently, the explanation for convergent evolution is not a matter of the restrictions of evolving systems themselves, but, as in the neo-Darwinian model of natural evolution, one which relies on the evolutionary analogy favoured by the similarity of adaptive environments:

> Grammatical universals exist, but I want to suggest that their existence does not imply that they are prefigured in the brain like frozen evolutionary accidents (…) they have emerged spontaneously and independently in each evolving language, in response to universal biases in the selection processes affecting language transmission. *They are convergent features of language evolution in the same way that the dorsal fins of sharks, ichthyosaurs, and dolphins are independent convergent adaptations of aquatic species.* (Deacon 1997: 115–116, our italics)[6]

It is illuminating to observe how Deacon (also Briscoe, and Evans and Levinson) seem to take for granted that the resemblance between legs, wings, eyes and fins in the animal kingdom can be explained by pure analogy, that is, as a product of independent (convergent) evolution. However, this is not the only conceivable path. It would certainly be unwise to rule out effects of this type in language change, but the recent development of evolutionary theory clearly makes it inadvisable to ignore the role of formal and invariant principles in the explanation of convergences.

Although it is a deep homology and not (at least apparently) a consequence of 'design laws of organic matter', the fact is that the evolution of those examples mentioned by Deacon and Briscoe (dorsal fins, wings and eyes) is one of the central arguments that can be used to oppose the adaptationist model. Thus, as described by Sampedro (2002: 119 et seq.), Gehring's group showed that the gene *Pax-6* (*eyeless* in Drosophila) is the *same* regulatory gene that controls the tens or hundreds of genes that form both arthropod and human eyes. This makes it clear that while evolution and selection have modified many of these genes to produce such incredibly different eyes as the compound eye of crustaceans and our own human eye, there is in fact a significant homology here. And the same can be said in general terms of the other body parts mentioned: wings, legs and fins have all traditionally been used as examples of evolutionary analogy, of convergent evolution, and thus as clear examples of how the medium shapes the adaptation of organisms, yet all have been revealed, so to speak, to have been invented at a given time in nature.

The conception of languages as external systems whose evolution is (more or less loosely) constrained by the human brain and human societies is valid as a metaphor, but it certainly can be detrimental to the naturalistic study of our language faculty. As noted by Kauffman:

> with the onset of full-blown evolutionism and Darwin's outlook on branching phylogenies, the very notion that biology might harbour ahistorical universal laws other than 'chance and necessity' has become simple nonsense. (Kauffman 1993: 5)

The same error could occur in linguistic theory if the neo-Darwinian model of the FCP is accepted. As Kauffman also argues, 'evolution, while destroying the idea of fixed species, simultaneously swept away the impetus to seek ahistorical laws of organic form' (Kauffman 1993: 3). But this very impetus, encouraged by the Chomskyan model, has gained ground in recent years, and its direction in this regard is akin to that of the bulk of biological science (see Benítez-Burraco and Longa 2010; Narita and Fujita 2010).

If there is, as suggested by the minimalist model, a universal internal syntax (derived from type 1 or type 3 factors, or a mixture of both), such a syntax may function as a source of 'order' in the 'organisms' that would be independent of, indeed immune to, 'natural selection' (i.e. language change). As suggested by the formal biological model proposed by Kauffman, part of the order that exists in the natural world exists 'not because of selection, but *despite* it' (Kauffman 1993: 16, original italics).

3.2 Language evolution and language change

Hereafter, partly to avoid ambiguity, we employ the term *language evolution* to refer to the evolution of the language faculty in the human species over geologic time, and the expression *language change* to refer to the change of languages over historical time (i.e. to processes such as those that led from Old English to current English or from Vulgar Latin to Spanish). This does not entail attributing qualitatively different values to the terms *evolution* and *change*, but only that the former refers to living organisms and the latter to cognitive organisms.

Nevertheless, when speaking of co-evolution there is a tendency to identify (in fact to mistake) the evolution of language as a human faculty with the change of languages as historical objects. This is not surprising since in the functional-cognitive paradigm the conception of the faculty of language is purely inductive, and thus the faculty of language in the species would evolve as a consequence of the individual evolution of languages. However, this confusion between linguistic change and language evolution has serious consequences for the scientific and naturalistic study of language.

In section 2.1 we suggested the appropriate correlates for the comparison between languages and species: I-languages are like organisms, and populations of similar I-languages are like species. This clarification is especially important if we want evolutionary theory to illuminate our understanding of language change. In our opinion, with few exceptions, the comparison has previously not been made in a satisfying way, in that it has not been addressed from a naturalistic point of view, as we have sought to do, but rather it has been raised as a memetic extension of the evolutionary process,[7] assuming then that languages are purely cultural objects.

The conclusion with which Darwin ends his reflection on the similarities between languages and species in *The Descent of Man* has not been sufficiently emphasized in these comparisons:

> From these few and imperfect remarks I conclude that the extremely complex and regular construction of many barbarous languages, is no proof that they owe their origin to a special act of creation. (Darwin, 1871: 114)

In our opinion, what Darwin is saying is that just as we need not postulate a designer to explain organisms' marvellous complexity and adaptation to their environment, we need not ascribe the marvellous complexity and functional perfection of languages to the will, desires or intentions of their speakers.

What matters to us now is that Darwin's intention was simply to establish an analogy, a comparison that would allow him to present his radical theory of the evolution of species by natural selection in a more acceptable way to the public, using the prestigious field of historical linguistics of the time as a means of illustration (see Alter 1999). Since then, with the notable exception of his contemporary August Schleicher (or, in our own time, Roger Lass 1997), the comparison between languages and species has been just that, a comparison, an illustrative analogy without any aim of true integration. And this is true not only of informal proposals, but also of many sophisticated developments of this analogy that have appeared since then, including some very influential ones, such as Greenberg (1992), Steels (1997), Nettle (1999), Kirby (1999), Croft (2000) and Mufwene (2002).

Of course, these proposals are valuable and have made interesting contributions to historical linguistics. The fundamental difference with respect to our own proposed correlation is that in the memetic conception of the analogy, natural evolution and language change are conceived of as two consecutive processes within a single dimension or vector. That is, linguistic evolution (language change) is seen as a continuation or even a part of natural evolution, which implies a confusion or perhaps an identification between the evolution of language as a human faculty and the historical evolution of languages. By contrast, the naturalistic conception of the comparison we have suggested (paradoxically) implies that linguistic evolution is not linked to nor is part of natural evolution, but is fully independent; it occurs under the same principles, but on a different scale or dimension. In this model, the evolution of language is totally independent of the evolution of languages. In this sense, once certain key parts of the modern FL arose in our species (e.g. due to a change in the structure of the brain), I-languages appeared and began to change, in 'historical' time. Since then, FL itself has functioned as another natural factor in restricting linguistic change. On the other hand, in the memetic model (corresponding to an inductive conception of the language faculty) the evolution of this faculty is the result of the evolution of languages.

As we have seen, the mere formulation of a theory of co-evolution between language and the brain implies such a dualistic conception according to which language is external to the brain (and not a property or a state of it). It also implies, even more strikingly, that language and the brain evolve independently, although with interactions. This, indeed, is the point of view defended by Evans and Levinson (although they do not mention Deacon):

> Coevolving sociocultural systems (languages) and their biological platforms (human brains) spur each other on [...] Once a coevolutionary approach is adopted [...] the presence of any universal feature calls for explanation in terms of two interacting components: the evolving semiotic system, and the evolving capacities of its users. (Evans and Levinson 2010: 2746)

But this dualist logic of the co-evolutionary model implies that languages function as adaptive environments for the brain, and that the brain functions as an adaptive environment for languages, since in the model the brain evolves to learn (and use) languages, and languages evolve in order to be learned (and used) by the brain.

It is not difficult to perceive the circularity here. Note that since brains are clearly prior to languages, then languages must have been produced by brains in the first instance (or less plausibly, they were copied from another species). Following this, languages would have been evolving (changing over time) and acquiring new emergent properties that, in turn, served as a new adaptive environment for brains themselves. Whence comes the structure of a language, other than as a result of constraints imposed by the brain itself, remains a mystery.

Since the FCP tends to reject the notion that human beings have a natural inclination towards language, and prefers to think of general learning and processing systems, it also favours a view according to which languages have done most of the adaptation in the co-evolutionary process, while the brain has been limited to achieving a general state. As we have already seen, Deacon suggests that 'the brain has co-evolved with respect to language, but languages have done the most of the adapting' (1997: 22).[8]

However, apart from a problem of circularity, the theory of language-brain co-evolution has other potentially critical implications for cognitive science. If we assume language-brain co-evolution and we also assume the great depth of the diversity of languages (the central premise of the programme presented by Evans and Levinson), then we have no choice but to assume that different languages might have produced different types of brains, that is, different types of faculty of (or capacity for) language in the same species. Far from rejecting this conclusion, Evans and Levinson seem to consider it seriously, even suggesting that the evolution of the 'human capacity for language' is still changing:

> There are also fundamental differences in the way language is implemented in brains (…) reflected in considerable individual differences in language performance, providing the raw material for ongoing evolution. If we are at all interested in language diversity and language variation, or the instantiation of language in the brain, we will need to bear a coevolutionary model of language in mind. (Evans and Levinson 2010: 2742)

It seems to follow, then, that any differences in the localization of language in individuals or groups of individuals could be explained because those individuals evolved in different linguistic contexts. It is hard to imagine a more extreme form of relativism.

With their emphasis on the conception of language as a cultural tool ('processes of cultural evolution hone languages into the marvelous instruments they are', Evans and Levinson 2010: 2742), they suggest that since 'the anatomy of the hand has coevolved with tool using' (*ibid.*), human anatomy would have coevolved with languages. One might ask then why the use of different types of tools did not cause differences in the anatomy and physiology of the hand, which appears essentially uniform in the species. There are two options: either the structure of the hand is not the result of the co-evolution with manual tools (which seems the most reasonable), or the hand evolved when it used a single type of tool. In such a case we would have to assume that if there are not different capacities for language, it is because the FL evolved when there was only one language or a restricted type of languages. In such a case, though, the evolution of the FL could not have been slow and gradual, as Evans and Levinson (2010: 2742) stipulate.

Consequently, we can say that co-evolutionary theory predicts than humans should be grouped according to various capacities for language, just as they are superficially grouped by the colour of their skin, the shape of their eyes, or the size of their noses. In fact, Evans and Levinson consider this possibility:

> The interaction of genes and language continue to evolve, as shown by the recent finding that language change has been channeled by population genetics in the last few thousands of years. (Evans and Levinson 2010: 2742)

They cite as evidence for this 'recent finding' the study of Dediu and Ladd (2007), according to which there is 'preliminary evidence that gene pools with certain biases in allele distribution are more likely to harbor languages of specific sorts' (Evans and Levinson 2009b: 480).[9] However, this study does not demonstrate that variation in certain genes has an influence on the development of tonal systems. Dediu and Ladd certainly suggest that these genetic differences might have an influence on language change, favouring tones:

> If differences in language and speech-related capacities are variable and heritable and if the genes involved have inter-population structure, it is likely that populations may differ subtly in some of these aspects, and that differences between populations could influence the way languages change through cultural evolution over time. (Dediu and Ladd 2007: 3)

Their study, though, is based on a statistical correlation and nothing else. Mark Lieberman's commentary on the study notes that it offers merely that, a statistical correlation, and does not prove a causal relationship between genetic variants and the occurrence of tones in languages, which might have many possible explanations:

> I suspect (though I haven't shown) that by jiggering the parameters of the simulation, you could get a frequency-distribution of geographical correlations rather like the one the Dediu and Ladd found, without assuming any meaningful connection at all between genes and linguistic traits. And of course there really are some connections, if only because of linguistic endogamy.[10]

Even if we can bridge the theoretical (and empirical) problem of a diverse natural capacity for language in humans, a model in which linguistic structure and complexity is the result of the individual evolution of languages cannot avoid the prediction that some languages may be more developed and evolved than others.

3.3 The language uniformity hypothesis

It is important to take into account that the two approaches we have reviewed make very different predictions about linguistic changes and, consequently, about the extent and depth of linguistic diversity.

According to a naturalist stance, linguistic change is severely restricted by formal requirements dictated by our biological specialization for language, what Pinker called *the language instinct*. This implies that human languages are essentially manifestations of the same system, as Chomsky claimed.

According to a culturalist standpoint, language change is constrained only by external factors (including our species' anatomy and physiology but also functional, social and cultural factors). This implies that languages can vary unpredictably and without limits, as stated by Martin Joos (1957).

According to these two different predictive profiles, it might seem that the so-called *language uniformity hypothesis* should be embraced only by the first group, but this is not the case. The language uniformity hypothesis (LUH) states that all languages have the same degree of development and that primitive languages therefore do not exist:

> It can be stated that one of the most important achievements of current linguistics is to have revealed that there are no primitive languages. (Moreno Cabrera 2000: 12, our translation)

The LUH is common in handbooks and introductions to linguistics regardless of their theoretical commitments (perhaps as a politically correct compensation for the denigrating assertions of the past). The LUH formulation as found in handbooks typically has several components:

- There are no primitive languages.
- All languages have the same degree of complexity.
- All languages can satisfy the same functions.
- All languages have the same dignity.
- All languages have, at an abstract level, the same structure.
- All languages have the same basic components.
- All languages offer the same degree of difficulty of acquisition as first languages, etc.

Although some of these assertions might be true or false independently of others (see Chapter 5 for a more detailed discussion), for now we will use the more extended version of the LUH that in some way embraces all of them: all existing languages present the same degree of evolution such that there are no languages that represent a previous or less developed state of human language.

Although they are subtly connected, the LUH and the so-called *uniformitarian principle* (UP) should not be seen as the same. The LUH is an empirical hypothesis, that is, an assertion regarding the existence or inexistence of certain objects, whereas the UP is a methodological principle of inquiry. In general, uniformitarianism assumes that the same natural laws and processes that operate in the universe now have always operated in the past and apply everywhere in the universe. This concept is usually stated as the idea that 'the present is the key to the past' because it holds that all things continue as they were from the beginning of the world.[11]

Early on in historical linguistics the UP was indeed assumed (see Lass 1997: 24 ff.), and Lass formulates the UP-derived position of historical linguistics thus:

> No linguistic state of affairs (structure, inventory, process, etc.) can have been the case only in the past. (Lass 1997: 28)

This principle, common to every historical science (be it physical, biological or linguistic) is based on the assumption that we should in principle discard reconstructions of the past that imply currently impossible states.[12]

Although the UP and the LUH are different, it is clear that in linguistics the methodological value of the former depends on the empirical reality of the latter. Also note that the UP is reliable if we identify the evolution of language (as a faculty) with *natural evolution*, not if we identify it with *linguistic evolution* (language change). This means that we should rely on the UP only if we neatly disconnect the evolution of the faculty of language from the historical change of languages.

In fact, the LUH extends naturally to documented ancient and extinct languages and, by virtue of the UP, even to reconstructed ones. There are good empirical reasons for this:

> This survey has uncovered no evidence that human language in general has changed since the earliest stage recoverable by the method used here. There is simply diversity, distributed geographically. The only thing that has demonstrably changed since the first stage of humanity is the geographical distribution of diversity. (Nichols 1992: 277)

Actually, the LUH poses two main problems: (i) whether it is in fact correct; and (ii) if it is indeed correct, why.

We do not think it excessively controversial to suggest that the vast majority of linguists accept (explicitly or implicitly) the LUH, and for this reason we are going to focus on question (ii).[13] This question is important because even though there is general consensus about the LUH, it is not clear if the LUH can be *deduced* from all approaches – and this is relevant because in science what matters is not only the outcome (apparently identical in this case, the LUH) but also how this result is obtained and whether it is predicted or not.

If we ask the countless supporters of the LUH why there are no primitive languages, we can expect two kinds of answers:

1. All current and historically recorded languages are the product of a unique language faculty, which is a result of the natural evolution of the species. Thus, every natural language spoken by a human being is restricted or conditioned by this faculty and cannot be primitive. Primitive languages disappeared when species with primitive language faculties disappeared.
2. All current and historically recorded languages have been evolving for tens of thousands of years, constrained by human processing and acquisition systems and by the cognitive and communicative functions they must fulfil. During this time, either modern human languages caused the extinction of primitive languages or the latter turned into the former.

It is easy to recognize a naturalist stance in answer 1, whereas a type-2 answer would seem to be the kind given by those who believe that the essential structure of languages is not biologically determined but is the outcome of the external pressures to which languages are subjected due to their use for communication and thought.

This approach underlies a good deal of functional linguistics (including the work of authors such as Givón, Comrie and Hawkins) and Deacon's co-evolutionary model (followed to a certain extent by authors such as Hurford, Kirby, Briscoe and even Evans and Levinson 2009a, b, 2010).

A type-1 answer might be considered *homological* – not, of course, because it is assumed that all languages come from a common ancestor (let's say *Proto-World*), but in the sense that it is assumed that all languages are variants of a common language faculty. Type-2 answers can be considered *analogical* theories of uniformity in the sense that it is each language's (long-term) historical evolution that would explain uniformity as confluence.

As pointed out previously, a relevant (and not always remarked upon) difference between both approaches with regard to the LUH is the degree of relevance conferred to linguistic change in the process of language evolution. For a homological theory, linguistic change has no functionally positive or negative effect; it is a process that is totally independent of the evolutionary emergence of language itself, an issue that has to do with the evolution of the human species. In contrast, for analogical theories, linguistic change is sensitive to these external factors and (although this is not always explicitly recognized) is part of the evolution of language.

In English, but not necessarily in other languages, the word *language* serves two functions: it represents particular languages (cf. French *langue* or Spanish *lengua*) and also language in general (cf. French *langage* or Spanish *lenguaje*). Thus, expressions such as *language evolution* or *language development* are inherently ambiguous. *Language evolution* can refer to both the historical changes in languages and the evolutionary process that created our special ability for language.[14] However, this 'unfortunate ambiguity' (Hurford 1992: 273) is not the only cause of frequent uncertainty regarding the use of expressions such as *language evolution* or *language development*. As we have suggested, for some authors there really is an authentic vagueness to the process of language evolution and the process of language change, which is of great importance in predicting the LUH. From this vague viewpoint, language evolves across the evolution of languages, which in turn are influenced by cultural evolution – whereas for 'homologists', languages do not 'evolve' but simply 'change'.

Consider, for example, the following excerpt from Comrie (2003):

> As a result of the recent development of grammaticalisation as a tool in historical linguistics it has been possible to develop a more general variant of internal reconstruction [...] that does enable us to come up with plausible hypotheses concerning earlier states of *language development*. (Comrie 2003: 249, emphasis added)

What is the author referring to here? Linguistic change or language evolution? From the evidence of this short passage, which includes a reference to the method of internal reconstruction and another to the concept of grammaticalization, it might appear that Comrie is referring to linguistic change in historical time. However, this is not the case, and in reality he is referring to both, simply because a purely historical conception of languages admits no precise way to of differentiating between the two phenomena. This, in our opinion, weakens the LUH notably.

Later, in the same article, our suspicions are confirmed:

> We can take grammaticalisation and base on it a kind of generalised internal reconstruction that gives us access to hypotheses concerning earlier stages of the language in question and by generalising our conclusions to earlier stages of language in general. (Comrie 2003: 249)

The reference to 'earlier stages of language in general' only has meaning as an allusion to the development of the faculty of language in the species. However, note that we are then admitting that linguistic change is directional and capable of changing the faculty of language (if recognized as such at all). Insofar as languages change at different rates and in different directions, we must also admit that the faculty of language is not uniform across the species and that, in fact, this faculty continues evolving among different groups.

Perhaps a schematic approach can clarify such differences. Figure 1 represents the evolutionary scenario that underlies the homological hypothesis:

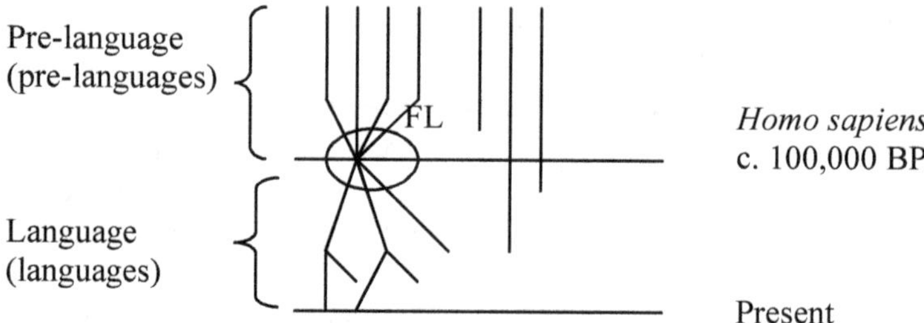

Figure 1: A 'homological' theory of language uniformity

Figure 1 is intended to show the emergence of FL as an evolutionary singularity (a 'bottleneck') from which the languages developed (as descending lines in the scheme) will be uniform, although we can allow for a certain amount of diversity as a result of linguistic change (which is shown by the usual family tree model). Before this evolutionary event (that we date 100,000 BP rather arbitrarily) there existed *pre-languages*: that is, those 'languages' used by ancestors of modern humans not yet equipped with a modern FL.[15] On the right side, we represent the process in other species (for example, the process for Neanderthal (pre)languages; the Neanderthals supposedly did not make the jump to modern language and became extinct c. 30,000 years ago).

Under the singularity marked with the ellipse, all human languages – modern or ancient, recorded or unrecorded, and regardless of their morphological or phonological complexity or their typological profile – will be modern languages.

The analogical scenario may be represented as follows:

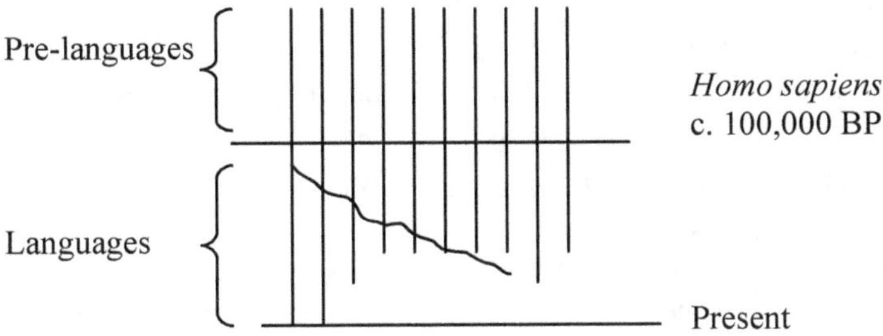

Figure 2: An 'analogical' theory of language uniformity

Figure 2 represents a scenario in which human biological evolution is a condition for language development but in which biology does not specify the structural properties of languages and hence there is no 'bottleneck'. Once languages crossed this frontier of human evolution, they began to acquire the structural complexity that now characterizes them through linguistic evolution.

The critical difference is that the horizontal line that separates cognitively modern humans and their ancestors (again dated 100,000 BP somewhat arbitrarily) does not coincide in time with the line that separates primitive languages and modern languages (represented by the descending irregular line in Figure 2). What this line is intended to show is the historical moment from which every historical lineage reaches the status of non-primitive language through the effect of linguistic change (evolution). This is a historical moment that may be different for each linguistic lineage and even for each language. The scheme includes the possibility that certain human languages (now extinct and unrecorded) did not successfully cross that frontier (e.g. the two lines on the right in the scheme).

Notably, the LUH also follows from this scenario, but in a rather different way. Under this approach, it is conceivable that some languages, although they are spoken by anatomically modern humans, continue to be primitive languages. Actually, this analogical model predicts that it is highly probable that during long time-spans, some anatomically modern human groups would speak primitive languages while others spoke modern languages.

According to this model, if there are no primitive languages today, it is because they have either become extinct or evolved historically towards modern status. In other words, in the analogical scenario, the LUH is contingent, even though it remains a highly probable theory.

It is now easier to understand why Comrie (2003) asserts that current studies on grammaticalization (which conceive of it as unidirectional) can offer insight into early states of human language and why he proposes to relativise the UP, excluding from it early language states. On such an approach, the transition between modern and primitive languages is gradual and merely historical. Language evolution (beyond a general biological endowment) limits itself to the evolution of languages; therefore, the reconstruction of the past of languages is equivalent to the reconstruction of primitive language.

In our opinion, this analogical scenario presents some empirical and methodological problems not found with the homological one: (i) the LUH is not predicted but only made probable, which gives credit to the possible existence of primitive or less developed human languages, something that does not seem to be empirically supported; (ii) linguistic change is predicted to be directional and progressive, and this claim is unsupported; (iii) the UP of historical linguistics is weakened; and (iv) an explanation of the evolution of language is rendered more difficult.

As for (iv), this objection is applicable to Deaconian, co-evolutionary explanations too. In Deacon's tradition, the ambiguity of expressions such as *language evolution* entails not only vagueness but also a deliberate mixture of the two meanings (this is precisely the meaning of 'co-evolution'). As we have seen, according to this model, the proper historical (cultural) evolution of languages was a factor in the adaptive biological evolution of the human brain. Note that if we assume this model to be correct, we need to assume also that all languages have reached a sufficient level of complexity to affect their users' brains (that is, to function as adaptive factors for the brain). However, the model then predicts that it is possible that there exist human groups with pre-human cognitive abilities: those whose languages did not evolve in the proper way.

The main difference between the analogical and homological models, then, is that only in the latter is a boundary provided by the assumption of a qualitative jump between classes of languages. The postulation of a biological evolutionary endowment that gives rise to a modern FL (even if it is 'minimal') allows us to establish a historical discontinuity between the classes of languages generated by evolutionarily differentiated FLs. The absence of this boundary in the analogical model causes us to attribute the LUH to the hypothesis that languages have converged into uniformity through the effect of the passage of time and external pressures. But note that the LUH is then not predicted (let us say it is a possibility, not a necessity), and hence we must entertain the possibility that this confluence has not occurred.

In fact, some authors explicitly consider such a possibility:

> Perhaps not all the languages that today exist in the world are in the same evolutionary stage. (Manjón and Luque 1997: 218, our translation)

Others have gone from the theoretical possibility to the claim of having discovered 'primitive languages' – that is, languages that because of diverse historical factors failed to reach the aforementioned boundary. Everett (2005) proposes as much for the Amazonian language Pirahã, which according to him lacks one of the (supposedly) central traits of human languages: recursion. In Pirahã, he argues, phrases cannot be embedded into other phrases (so that there are no subordinated clauses), interpreting this as a cultural constraint on grammar, and thus presenting it as empirical evidence against a naturally determined FL and in favour of relativism.

Nevins *et al.* (2009) forcefully refute this analysis. In his reply to them, Everett (2007) stresses that he does not mean that the minds of Pirahã speakers are limited in the use of recursion or the use of recursive languages generally, hence orientating the issue for him on the analogical model; what Everett is implying, then, is that some of the languages in Figure 2 did not become extinct but rather still exist today (as in Figure 3). This is a denial of the LUH.

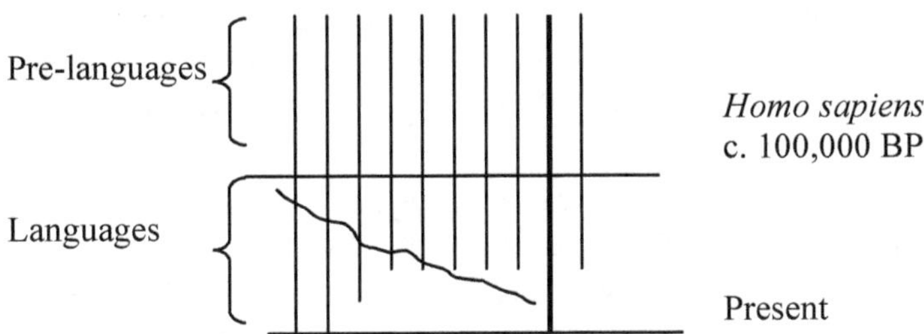

Figure 3: A negation of the Language Uniformity Hypothesis

The scheme here is the same as before except for the bold line representing a language that has not reached the critical evolutionary boundary between primitive and modern languages as of the present time. However, what really matters is that under an analogical approach, the difference between denying or supporting the LUH is purely accidental; it depends on whether languages have evolved properly.

It is true that the homological model smacks of circularity insofar as modern languages are defined as those spoken by modern humans. However, in the final analysis, this is the crucial matter: is the boundary between pre-language and language just cultural, or is it biological?

To argue that it is both things (as in co-evolution theories) amounts to saying that it is cultural, inasmuch as, if the historical process does not occur, then neither does the transition. In making such a claim, however, we would presume that there exist modern human beings that nevertheless speak primitive languages – that is, classes of languages produced by ancestral language abilities that for contingent reasons (social or cultural) have not had sufficient time to evolve in the expected way.[16] We believe that this is the only foundation on which the emerging new and radical relativism can be constructed, and it is a rather weak one (see later 5.4).

Our conclusion, then, is that the empirical robustness of the LUH can be seen as an argument in favour of the biological theory of the uniformity of languages.

3.4 How to understand language change

3.4.1 A mistaken view of natural language evolution

As we have noted in previous sections, the conception of natural languages as cultural objects induces a memetic view of the evolution (change) of natural languages. Often, this conception inherits an excessively neo-Darwinian view of evolution which, if inadequate for natural organisms, it is certainly so for natural languages. We might recall here Darwin's wise remarks after quoting Müller on the success of the (allegedly) fittest sounds or words (see 1.3).

Bichakjian's Darwinist view of language evolution (Bichakjian 2002) is an example of a deeply flawed work which adopts this way of thinking. His arguments are worth reviewing here because they are either implicitly or explicitly made by many linguists with different theoretical backgrounds. Bichakjian uses linguistic features as units subject to Darwinian evolution, making the point as follows:

> Language evolution will therefore be a process that replaces an existing feature with a new one that requires a smaller expenditure of energy while providing at least equal and preferably better functional capabilities. (Bichakjian 2002: 94)

Such an approach to Darwinist evolution amounts to saying that there are at least two particular functional goals driving the evolution of the species: the law of least effort and the law of functional optimization. No doubt both factors can exert a certain influence in the local, short-term process of adaptation to a certain environment. However, this is not the essence of Darwinian evolution, which is based on random variation and natural selection.

Protective coloration in animals provides a good illustration of Darwinian evolution. Some animals have a skin colour similar to their surroundings. The Darwinian reason for this feature has nothing to do with a goal-oriented natural selection. Animals do not change their skin colour *in order to* avoid predators; this would be Lamarckian evolution. Natural selection can work because, first, there is a certain range of variation in the skin colour in a particular species; in some cases, specific individuals may by pure accident have a skin colour very similar or identical to that of their surroundings. These individuals will have far greater scope for avoiding predators and hence of survival, and as a consequence they will be more likely to reproduce. Another extreme case of this evolutionary mechanism is represented by the *phasmatodea* insect order, popularly known as *stick insects*. The body shape of these insects replicates the forms of sticks and leaves, and the bodies of some species are even covered in mossy outgrowths; in addition, some of the species have the ability to change colour in order to match that of their surroundings.

It makes no sense to say that a particular skin colour or body shape, as a biological feature, is *replaced* by another if it is more efficient in a particular environment; this is only a metaphorical way of speaking. Rather, random physical variation happens to produce a particular skin colour or body shape that has protective properties in a particular environment. Of course, possible radical changes in that environment could render such body features completely useless for survival. As a consequence, it can be said that there is nothing intrinsically good or advantageous in a particular body feature subjected to random variation.

The idea that natural selection *replaces* a particular skin colour or body shape in order to provide the species with an opportunity for survival is an *a posteriori* teleological view and, therefore, does not describe adequately how natural selection works in the Darwinian sense. But this is exactly what Bichakjian does when speaking about the selection of specific linguistic features.[17] In addition, linguistic features are not individuals, let alone species, and it therefore makes no sense to maintain that there exists competition among different linguistic features.

Chapter five of Bichakjian's book is devoted to the so-called evolution of linguistic features. His main thesis here is that complexity of form is less evolved than complexity of features:

> The foregoing chapter tried to show that complexity of form and complexity of function are two separate entities, and that the one should not mistake the former, which is a likely characteristic of archaic features, for the latter, which is normally indicative of more advanced states of development. (Bichakjian 2002: 109)

He refers to a putative universal principle governing language evolution, what he calls *Humboldt's Universal*. This universal stipulates a bi-unique relationship between form and function and can be formulated in the following way: one form/one meaning. Bichakjian explains in this way the loss of inflection in languages such as Latin and Anglo-Saxon, giving rise to modern languages such a French, Spanish and English. These languages lost the inflectional endings of nouns having a synthetic character and replaced them with analytical constructions using prepositions:

> In English, for instance, the various functions of the ablative are expressed with prepositions such as *from, at, in, on, by, with,* and *than*, each of them having a measure of polysemy (cf. *the gentleman **from** Richmond,* but also *the flowers are **from** John; **at** the station*, but also ***at** midnight*; ***in** the room* and ***in** the evening; to be hit **by** a car, to travel **by** car*, and *to drive **by** night; to write **with** a pen* and *to go out **with** a friend*). (Bichakjian 2002: 139, italics and bold face by the author)

This is a case of language change, and it is clear that historical change does not work in this way, that is, by replacing a linguistic feature with another. For linguistic change to be possible it is necessary for the process to commence from a state of grammatical variation; moreover, the different components of grammatical competence are related to each other in very complex ways, so that a slight change in one component can originate long-range changes in other components. This is typical of a complex adaptive system, in which changes cannot be explained by one single cause or principle. Lightfoot, in Chapter 5 of his book on the development of language (Lightfoot 1999), explores the syntactic consequences of the loss of case over the course of the history of English:

> It is true that grammars are formed in a child in accordance with the prescription of the linguistic genotype; consequently, they are economical and beautiful in ways imposed by UG. However, they are also shaped by the demands of haphazard experience, and this makes them historically contingent. [...] If the linguistic experience of some children shifts a little, there may be dramatic consequences: the resulting grammar may generate a very different set of sentences. Furthermore, the shift may have a domino effect. [...] In particular, we shall see the loss of case endings may have catastrophic effects, entailing changes – sometimes odd-looking changes – in the syntax. (Lightfoot 1999: 111)

He emphasizes variation as an important condition of language change:

> A striking property of the loss of the old patterns is its gradualness. The morphological case system was lost over the period from the

> tenth to the thirteenth century. What this means for us is that the two grammars coexisted for several hundred years. (Lightfoot 1999: 135)

In addition he observes that morpho-syntactic change cannot be seen as a simple substitution of a certain linguistic feature, but as the transformation of a complex system of morpho-syntactic relations requiring a fine-graded linguistic analysis:

> If we view the oblique morphological cases as the realization of abstract inherent Cases, then we can see that the loss of the morphological cases entailed a range of syntactic changes. These include not only the new split genitives discussed in the last section, but also the loss of the so-called psych-verbs and the rise of nominative-accusative forms. I have offered a minimal account of the changes: the oblique cases were lost and ceased to realize the abstract, inherent Cases. On the theory that I have sketched, this entailed a variety of surface manifestations, and we have an explanation for why certain phenomena clustered in the way they did. (Lightfoot 1999: 136)

The mistaken teleological view adopted by Bichakjian is evident once we realize the chaotic nature of language change:

> Grammatical change is highly contingent – chaotic in the technical sense. Linguists can offer satisfying explanations of changes in some instances, but there is no reason to expect to find a predictive theory of change, offering long-term, linear predictions. (Lightfoot 1999: 259)

In Chapter 7 of his book, Bichakjian studies the evolution of writing, trying to apply a Darwinian perspective to it. But this cannot be done, since writing is a cultural, not a natural phenomenon, and therefore does not evolve by natural selection in a Darwinian way. Cultural phenomena evolve in a Lamarckian way; their evolution is subjected to certain goals and tenets consciously and purposely sought by people, and their modifications are often planned beforehand in accordance with such goals.

For Bichakjian, the key factor in accounting for the evolution of writing lies in the supposed change from perceptual reproduction to conceptual representation:

> The gradual shift from perceptually-suggested pictures to the most advanced form of conceptually-inspired speech transcription is provided by the succession of scripts that extends from the Egyptian hieroglyphs to the Greek alphabet. (Bichakjian 2002: 223)

This view of the evolution of writing is essentially wrong. Such a supposed evolution only concerns the form of the graphemes, and not the structure of the writing system. A clear case in point is Egyptian writing. This writing system developed three different scripts: Hieroglyphic, Hieratic and Demotic. The fundamental script is the first, from which Hieratic and Demotic were developed as cursive derivatives (Ritner 1996: 73). The Hieroglyphic script contains pictographic graphemes, perceptually-suggested pictures in Bichakjian terms. But from the point of view of the writing system, Egyptian writing is a logographic system with a clear phonographic (consonantal) basis (Ritner 1996: 73–74). Hence the pictograms of the Hieroglyphic script do not represent images or ideas, but full-fledged words. The other two scripts (Hieratic and Demotic) are not pictographic from the point of view of their appearance, but they realize exactly the same writing system:

> Although the pictorial appearance of the individual hieroglyphic signs of monumental inscriptions was highly stylized in the hieratic book script (mid-second millennium BCE) and completely lost in the popular demotic script (seventh century BCE), these changes in the outer form of Egyptian writing did not result in any functional changes concerning the inner form of the writing system. (Coulmas 1996: 138–139)

Bichakjian fails to make the important distinction between a writing system and a script. Over the course of the history of writing, the same writing system has been materialized frequently in different scripts; one thing is the type of writing system, and an entirely different thing is the form or visual configuration of the script. Script forms are heavily dependent on the material support of the writing system: monumental scripts tend to present a quadrangular shape, but leaf or paper writing usually shows a rounded shape. This is a case of script adaptation to the writing surface and has no obvious influence on the evolution of writing systems.

On the other hand, the transition of Egyptian hieroglyphs to the Greek alphabet has nothing to do with a supposed evolution from perceptual images to conceptually-inspired speech-transcription, as Bichakjian claims. Egyptian writing has, as we have noted, a clear consonantal basis, showing that it does indeed involve speech-transcription. The progressive phonetization of logographic writing systems that can be observed in the history of writing has to do with the effects of borrowing. When an illiterate community borrows a logographic writing system from another community and their respective languages are not genetically related, the original writing system experiments a process of phonetization: this occurred for example in the borrowing by the Akkadians of the cuneiform Sumerian writing to transcribe their language, and also in the use of Chinese writing by the Japanese to transcribe the Japanese language, which gave rise to its two syllabic writings.

3.4.2 In what sense is language evolution cultural evolution?

In her comprehensive survey of the evolutionary approaches to language variation and change, Rosenbach (2008: 23) considers that language evolution is an example of biological evolution and that language change is an example of cultural evolution. First, as we have argued above, it is clear that we must distinguish between the evolution of the language faculty, directly related to the evolution of the human species, and language change, this being a wholly different phenomenon. Nevertheless there are general aspects of language change that could be analysed in terms of biological evolution on a view called *Universal Darwinism*:

> Both are developmental processes, however, and in recent years it has been claimed that there are general evolutionary processes (such as variation, selection, and self-replication) underlying *any* historical evolved, complex system, subsuming both biological and cultural evolution [...] a view which has come to be known as UNIVERSAL DARWINISM. Under this view, language change may be regarded as an instance of cultural evolution and as being subject to the same general evolutionary mechanisms driving biological evolution. (Rosenbach 2008: 24, italics and capitals as in the original)

The use of the expression *cultural evolution* can be confusing here, in that it suggests again a memetic approach to languages. Of course, natural languages originate and develop within a society, thus within a culture, but they do so in a spontaneous, purposeless and non-intentional way; they are not intentional cultural constructions, artificially created by humans by means of explicit conventions. In this sense, natural languages are not cultural objects or constructs. Of course, there exist culturally determined languages: these are what we here call *cultivated languages*, originating by an intended, purposeful and goal-oriented elaboration of natural languages.

Darwin referred to this particular point in his brief review of the evolutionary aspects of natural languages:

> But it is assuredly an error to speak of any language as an art, in the sense of its having been elaborately and methodically formed. (Darwin 1871: 114)

Darwin is absolutely right. Natural languages have not been formed through an explicit cultural elaboration by their speech communities; English and French have not been established by means of conscious actions on the part of some members of their respective speech communities.[18]

As Darwin noted in his reflection cited in Section 3.2 (which we repeat here), the apparent complexities and regularities of natural languages do not demonstrate a purposeful elaboration of linguistic structure:

> From these few and imperfect remarks I conclude that the extremely complex and regular construction of many barbarous languages, is no proof that they owe their origin to a special act of creation. (Darwin 1871: 114)

In this sense, it can be said that natural language variation and change is a natural and not a cultural phenomenon. Therefore, language variation and change is not directly related to cultural evolution, as will be argued in the next chapter.

This does not mean that there is no relation at all between language variation and change and cultural factors. Indeed, social and cultural factors can affect in different ways the evolution of natural languages in the Darwinian sense. Their CAS character explains this in a straightforward way. As complex adaptive systems, natural languages (in the sense of populations of I-languages) respond in several ways to the social and cultural influences of the speech community in which they exist.[19] But they do so in a spontaneous, non-intentional way, and therefore such interactions do not alter the non-cultural or natural essence of language variation.

In order to illustrate this point, a proposal by Hale (2007) proves extremely useful. He postulates a post-grammatical processor, developed to modify in a certain way the grammatical products of the natural linguistic competence of the individual in order to adapt to certain intentionally accepted goals. Hale (2007: 43) maintains that in the first steps of the learning of a foreign language, in order to produce a sentence in the new language, students apply a series of rules by which they replace in turn the lexical elements of the corresponding sentence in their own native tongue by the lexical items of the new language. These word-for-word replacements are not possible grammatical rules according to the principles of Universal Grammar, and therefore cannot be a part of the grammatical competence. Such rules apply post-grammatically once a sentence has been produced by the natural grammatical competence of the individual. They belong to that post-grammatical processor. Hale suggests that something very similar occurs when speakers of a non-standard linguistic variety try, in a conscious way, to produce sentences in which dialectal or non-standard grammatical features are replaced by the corresponding standard features. In these cases, the post-grammatical processor carries out the necessary changes:

> Extensive use of this postprocessor can make it very fast and very efficient, but because of the nature of its operations, it will never *become* a grammar. The fact that my output, when using this post-processor, has changed, perhaps dramatically, cannot therefore be taken as an instance of 'change' in the historical linguistic sense. (Hale 2007: 44)

All this implies that social factors (affecting E-language) do not exert a direct influence on the natural grammatical competences of individuals. People resort to a non-natural linguistic ability (the post-grammatical processor) in order to adjust their grammatical performance to a certain prestigious model of speech, a clear E-language phenomenon. There is, therefore, no direct interaction between grammatical competence and social factors.

However, this artificially modified performance has important effects on the process of natural language acquisition. As children cannot directly access the grammatical competence of adults, they develop their grammatical competence on the basis of the linguistic performance of adult members of the speech community, determining many aspects of E-languages (Lightfoot 2006: 66–86). As this performance can be the result of applying the post-grammatical processor, they can develop grammatical competences differing at certain points from the natural grammatical competence of adults, so that their natural grammatical competence may have some of the grammatical features of the more prestigious language variety. From a superficial point of view, a social factor (prestige) has thus caused a grammatical change in a natural language. But if we take a closer look at Hale's view in applying it to our scenario, it is clear that this change is a natural process and not a cultural process, since it is based in the biologically conditioned process of natural language acquisition. A social factor has caused a non-natural response in the adults, in the sense that the response is not necessarily driven by the principles of Universal Grammar and involves non-linguistic cognitive abilities. But the mechanism by which children naturally develop their grammatical competence is not changed at all by that social factor. Children will never acquire the word-for-word replacement rules used by the adults to modify their linguistic output in certain ways: they will build up a new grammatical competence according to the principles of Universal Grammar and other third-factor effects (see 2.4.1), on the basis of that intentionally modified linguistic output. So, social factors in language change (most notably in grammatical change diffusion) have to do with E-languages, and Hale's post-grammatical processor can determine some of the E-languages characteristics.

The complex interaction between E-language and I-Language in linguistic change has been described by Lightfoot (1999, 2006). The following is very illustrative of this relationship:

> So adults modify their speech through changes in their use of their natively acquired system and that changes the ambient E-language. Slight changes in E-language may have crucial effects on how the next generation of I-languages develops in the brains of young children within the critical period. The usual flux of E-language most commonly does not affect the way in which children acquire their I-language – for long periods structural shifts may not happen – but from time to time E-language may change in a way that triggers the growth of a new grammar. In Chapter 4, we developed a model whereby children scan their environment for speech that expresses grammatical cues and they develop their individual I-language accordingly. If E-language crosses some threshold such that the cues are expressed differently and a different I-language is triggered, we have a different kind of change, a new I-language. (Lightfoot 2006: 163).

This results into a historical cycle involving I-languages and E-languages, which is characterized by Lightfoot in the following way:

> New E-language may cue new I-languages, which, in turn, entail new E-Language. We have new languages at different levels, children and adults are involved in different ways, and we find never-ending cycles of change, driven ultimately by the fact that people use their grammars creatively, expressively, and idiosyncratically, so that speech is highly individual within the bounds of shared I-language … and, of course, shared UG; I-language is shared within a speech community and UG is shared by all humans, across the species.
>
> This means that there are coexisting grammars within the brains of some individuals, who have multiple competencies. That, in turn, entails oscillation between certain fixed points, particular I-languages and not random variation. (Lightfoot 2006: 164)

In addition to individual and idiosyncratic use of an I-language, we must add the different types of social elaborations of E-languages that can also enter the E-language/I-language interactive circle in language change. Lightfoot notes that an individual can also have multiple I-languages serving as fixed points in the dynamics of I-language variation and change.

Notes

1. Note that the prefix *anti-* has scope on *neo-Darwinist*, and not only on *Darwinist*. See Gould (2002) for a detailed discussion.
2. As Benítez-Burraco and Longa (2010) point out, Mayr noted more than 40 years ago that 'much that has been learned about gene physiology makes it evident that the search for homologous genes is quite futile except in very close relatives' (*apud* Benítez-Burraco and Longa 2010: 310). These authors identify this view as 'different genes for different animals', and also note that 'for more than a century, biologists had assumed that different types of animals were genetically constructed in completely different ways', while 'Evo-Devo has shown (…) that such a contention was unjustified' (Benítez-Burraco and Longa 2010: 310).
3. 'The earliest modern human remains date back to about 200,000 BP, and outside Africa date from only 100,000 years or so ago. If that is the date of the great diaspora, there has been relatively little time for diversification' (Evans and Levinson 2009b: 477).
4. See the works collected in Briscoe, ed. (2002) for an overview of the model. Hurford (2002) calls this tradition the 'expression/induction' model.
5. Evans and Levinson themselves suggest that the model offered is intended to determine 'how much design must be in the organism and how much design can evolve on purely cultural grounds' (Evans and Levinson 2010: 2734) and they definitely opt for the second option.
6. In a similar vein, Briscoe states: 'such historical pathways can be stereotypical responses to similar pressures arising in unrelated languages, *in much the same way that eyes and wings have evolved independently in different lineages many times*, without the need to posit a substantive theory of such changes or to see them as deterministic' (Briscoe 2002: 13, my italics). Of course, Evans and Levinson share this view: 'the distribution of attested structural types across the design space reflects the likelihoods of the evolutionary pathways that would engender them, rather than specific constraints on the structures themselves' (Evans and Levinson 2010: 2734)
7. According to Merriam-Webster Dictionary a *meme* is 'an idea, behavior or style that spreads from person to person within a culture'. A meme acts as a unit for carrying cultural ideas, symbols or practices, which can be transmitted from one mind to another. The word *meme* is a shortening (modelled on *gene*) of *mimeme* ('something imitated' in Ancient Greek). See Dawkins (1976).
8. Note that otherwise it is not easy to distinguish this position from the traditional generative conception of UG as a *Language Acquisition Device*. Smith and Kirby (2008: 283) pose the dilemma clearly: 'There are two possible sources of structure in language: biological evolution of the language faculty, or cultural evolution of language itself', and they take the second.
9. To which they add: 'We are not dealing, then, with an invariant machine at

all, but with a biological system whose evolution has relied on keeping variance in the gene pool' (Evans and Levinson 2009b: 480).

10. In http://itre.cis.upenn.edu/~myl/languagelog/archives/004554.html (accessed 09.20.2010) Dediu and Ladd do not contradict these conclusions, and recognize the lack of correlation (according to contemporary knowledge), declaring that 'it's certainly true, as Mark says, that our geographical correlations would mean more if they had proceeded from some experimental demonstration of some sort of genetically linked, language-related, cognitive/behavioral/perceptual difference'. In the context of our discussion, the motivation to publish their study is not without interest: 'But given the widespread assumption (rooted in the Boasian tradition, but with a significant contemporary boost from Chomsky) that the human language faculty is absolutely uniform across the species, it's very unlikely that we would have been able to get funding to look for such a difference first. So we started by doing something we could do on our own without such support, namely testing the apparent correlation.'
11. The principle is commonly attributed to geologist Charles Lyell. The subtitle of his influential *Principles of Geology* (1830) sets it out clearly: 'An attempt to explain the former changes of the Earth's surface by reference to causes now in operation'.
12. Comrie (1992: 204) provides a rather clear example: because all attested languages have consonants, a reconstruction must be rejected if it posits an ancestor language that has no consonants.
13. But see Chapter 5 for some possible exceptions.
14. Normally the term *evolution* biases the interpretation towards the natural process. We use the term *evolution* without meaning 'progression', 'advancement' or 'improvement', either in the biological or in the linguistic context. In fact, we use the term simply to mean 'change'.
15. We use the terms *pre-languages* (and *pre-language*) instead of Bickerton's (1990) classic term *protolanguage* because the latter has its own use and tradition in historical linguistics (as in *proto-Germanic*, etc.). Besides, we do not mean that modern languages are historical descendents of pre-languages (they could be, of course, but according to the model adopted, that would be irrelevant).
16. Even Comrie, when he suggests distinguishing between 'the human language potential' and the 'realisation of the human language potential' (Comrie 2003: 250) is obliquely introducing an anti-unformitarian stance.
17. For a critique of such arguments in historical linguistics see Lass (1997) and Mendívil-Giró (2009).
18. Written standard languages, as cultural elaborations, originated precisely in this way.
19. Labov's detailed monograph (Labov 2001) is entirely devoted to this topic.

4 Characterizing cultivated languages

As we have seen in the previous chapters, human societies produce different types of cultural language elaborations. The results of such elaborations are what we call *cultivated languages*, a special type of E-Languages. The standard languages of Europe are a specific type of cultivated language. But they are not the only kind of outcome of elaboration processes. In this chapter, we will summarize and briefly characterize the main types of cultivated languages.

It is important to note that the language elaboration activity producing cultivated languages uses real language production as its source, that is, the process involves the elaboration of E-languages, and the outcome is an elaborated E-language. In other words, they do not arise as a result of a direct modification of natural grammatical competence (I-language). The reason for this is very simple: I-languages cannot be directly accessed and modified, with only certain language areas of production – vocabularies, texts, discourses – capable of being submitted to an intentional, goal-oriented modification towards the creation of a cultivated language. Modern standard languages and literary languages are usually developed on the basis of written texts, and thus are not elaborations of I-languages, but rather specific types of E-language.

4.1 A typology of cultivated languages

In human societies we find two main types of language elaboration. The first of these, the esoteric type, is focused on the relationships, customs or beliefs characteristic of that society and tries to adjust and adapt a natural language in certain ways to reflect those inner functions or properties of the community in question. Such elaborations make natural languages more opaque, complex and difficult to interpret without an appropriate background. Literary language is a good example. Oral or written literary works can only be properly understood with reference to the cultural traditions in which they are produced: these traditions include literary genres and a special language deviating to some extent from everyday speech.

Let us briefly review the two main types of this kind of E-language elaboration, which we will call 'esoteric language elaboration'. One common example is ritual and cryptic language, typical of many human communities and societies. The language accompanying rituals is usually not normal everyday speech. It deviates from it in certain specific and particular ways not only in terms of pronunciation, but also in the selection of lexical items, of syntactic constructions and figures of speech. This type of language can only be learned by guided instruction and very often it is only the initiated who knows and can use it on specific occasions. Examples of this CL type abound throughout the world. For example, Yelle discusses the research of Malinowski into Kiriwinian spells:

> These spells exhibited a 'coefficient of weirdness' that came from their use of archaisms and apparently meaningless forms, onomatopoeias, repetitive and rhythmic chanting, extensive metaphors, and allusions to myth. (Yelle 2006: 635)

Another clear case of a type of the cryptic elaboration of a natural language is reported by Evans (2010):

> William Thurston studied 'esoterogeny' – the engendering of difference and linguistic obscurity – with Anem speakers on the island of New Britain, off the New Guinea mainland. He found that 'esoterogenic' languages tend to streamline pronunciation in ways that make the overall structure harder to see, comparable to saying *dja* por *didja* from *did you* in English. They replace clear regular relationships with 'suppletive' (totally irregular) ones, revealing in alternations like *good:better* at the expense of the more transparent *big:bigger* style. They have huge numbers of opaque idioms, of the *kick the bucket* type, and entrench prescriptive traditions that limit the flexibility of language: 'you must speak this way to be a member of our community!' They also elaborate terminology to make subtle distinctions, and speakers take pride in the greater richness of their language than the neighboring language of Lusi in this regard. (Evans 2010: 13)

As we can see in this passage, the intentional elaboration of a natural language here has an important social meaning and is based on a prescriptive tradition that is also evident in the written standard languages of industrialized societies. Such types of linguistic elaboration are found in different social groups, as Thurston observes:

> During Thurston's research on Anem he found that 'some of the boys had devised a competitive word game aimed at exposing one another's ignorance for an obscure vine or bush; in order to keep ahead, boys were asking older people, secretively, for words they would use to try tricking other boys.' All these features conspire

> to maximize difference between one language and its neighbors. (Evans 2010: 13)

Dixon (2002: 91 ff.) describes several speech styles of aboriginal Australian languages. These styles are obtained through certain cultural elaborations of everyday natural language. Initiation styles are used exclusively between initiated men and are taught to youths during initiation. A notable example is the Damin style of the Australian Lardil language. This cultivated language has about 150 lexemes with a very wide range of meanings, and also has a different phonological system. It is said to have been invented by an ancestor of the tribe. As such it is an extreme case of a culturally elaborated language serving ritual purposes.

In the ritual elaboration of Australian aboriginal languages, the lexicon, the most salient property of a natural language (at least for normal speakers) is typically subjected to various modifications. In extreme cases, the vocabulary of the natural language is completely replaced in ritual, avoidance or respect styles. For example, in Yidinj and Dyirbal every verb, adjective and noun has a different form in the normal and special styles, although the grammatical forms do not differ (Dixon 2002: 93). However, in both these languages the special styles have a smaller vocabulary. For example, whereas in the everyday style there are different names for the various types of ant, there is just one noun for 'ant' in the avoidance style. The form of the words in the avoidance style often is obtained by means of the addition or subtraction of a syllable or by means of a phonetic transformation of the corresponding everyday word. For example, the Jirrbal word *banaga* 'return' in the everyday language is replaced by *walaga* in the avoidance style (Dixon 2002: 94–95). Some words may also be borrowed from a neighbouring language or dialect. There is also a special speech style, the 'mourning style', using for grieving over a recently deceased relative and extolling their virtues (Dixon 2002: 95).

In North American Indian languages several special speech styles with characteristic intonation, vocabulary, grammatical forms, formulaic expressions and special textual structure can also be found (Mithun 1999: 272–294). Ceremonial styles, for example, may be characterized by special prosody, vocabulary, metaphor, repetition, and strong textual structure (Mithun 1999: 285). Ceremonial vocabulary is generally more archaic than that of colloquial language and is transmitted from generation to generation with little alteration. In addition, it is typically characterized by euphemism, metaphor and circumlocutions. Thus, in Wintu shaman speech a periphrastic expression *tuwinherestopi* 'used for that which is seen ahead' is employed with the meaning 'eyes'; in Zuni, 'frogs' are referred to in sacred songs as *woliye tinan k'ayapa*, literally 'several are in a shallow container' (Mithun 1999: 287).

We also find special types of language for religious purposes in European societies. An example can be found in the traditional version of the *Lord's Prayer* in which we can find unusual words (including a Hebrew word at the end) and expressions and unusual morphology and syntax:

Our Father, Who art in heaven
Hallowed be Thy Name;
Thy kingdom come,
Thy will be done,
on earth as it is in heaven.
Give us this day our daily bread,
and forgive us our trespasses,
as we forgive those who trespass against us;
and lead us not into temptation,
but deliver us from evil. Amen.

Other examples include the case of contemporary Armenian, which is not used in the celebration of mass, ancient Armenian or Grabar being preferred, and the Muslim practice of praying in a Classical Arabic, which, according to the country, is either completely or partially different from the mother tongue of those at prayer.

All these linguistic elaborations having a ritual, ceremonial or religious purpose, and produce discourse and texts spoken or written in an artificially modified language that is different – sometimes very different – from the natural language on which they are based. And it is important to note that in all known human societies some sort of linguistic elaboration for ritual, ceremonial or religious purposes can be found.

The second universal type of esoteric language elaboration is poetic or literary language.[1] All known human societies develop certain linguistic elaborations with poetic goals. These elaborations of natural languages are culturally determined and are usually characterized as verbal art. Linguistic form tends to be the focus of attention here; grammatical form is submitted to certain modifications or regulations in order to provoke a special effect on the audience. For example, the repetition and parallelism of sounds, words and sentences is characteristic of the poetic language in many different societies and cultures. Metrical rules are another case in point, and different metrical patterns are found in a wide variety of poetic traditions. These rules subject the normal speech to special constraints, producing unusual discourses and texts. Such products constitute the base of this special type of E-language: the so-called poetic or literary language.

In songs, known in virtually every human community, musical, metrical and phonological, morphological and syntactic forms interact in intricate ways to produce a special type of discourse deviating in significant ways from normal everyday speech. Whereas written poetic language is a special type of E-language, characteristic only of certain type of societies, songs are a form of cultural elaboration of natural language present in every human community, no matter if it is literate or not. In fact, written literature almost always derives ultimately from purely oral literature. And all human societies possess some form of oral literature, including those in which literacy developed a long time ago.

The second, the exoteric type of natural language elaboration, often aims at simplifying a natural language in order to make it easier to understand and interpret by people not fully acquainted with the customs and uses of a community, for example children or foreigners. Language simplification is a constant activity in many communities when trying to contact other communities with a different language.

Two main factors provoke this type of language modification. One is determined by the willingness to communicate with members of a linguistic community who are acquiring its natural language, notably children. In a largely spontaneous way, adults modify certain aspects of their speech to make it more understandable to children, sometimes known as *motherese* or *baby talk*. In English, for example, it is characterized by high pitch, grammatically simple utterances, special words, repetitions and restriction of topics. Most of these changes are made in order to simplify a given NL. Hence, these modifications lead to an elaborated, cultivated language.

The second factor here is related to the need for communication between people whose language is not mutually intelligible. In certain circumstances, such as in trading relations, members of different linguistic communities need to understand each other. In order to do that, they may make a series of simplifications and accommodations of their languages in a generally spontaneous way by shortening and mixing the vocabularies, the morphology and the syntax of their respective languages. When such circumstances recur with a certain frequency, pidgin languages can emerge. Pidgins are a very common example of spontaneous language elaboration through simplification, and are usually created by adults whose natural languages are not mutually intelligible, but where there is a need for understanding.

Pidgins and artificial international languages (like Esperanto) are in fact two extremes of the same continuum of language elaboration by simplification. The pidgin extreme corresponds to a mini-language with a reduced vocabulary serving a very small range of situations and originating in a more or less spontaneous way:

> [T]he principal external factor giving rise to *(early) pidgins* was the pressing need […] for a medium of interethnic communication. […] Early pidgin creators, then, were typically adults with their own

> native tongues and with limited practice in the evolving pidgin, initially using it in limited (and limiting) interaction. (DeGraff 1999: 5)

It is important to note that pidgins, however spontaneously they emerge, represent a conscious act by adults towards mutual understanding in specific situations. They have a definite purpose and are based on a generally conscious, partial elaboration of two or more natural languages. Therefore, they are not natural languages, yet neither are they basic or primitive languages, but rather cultural products artificially devised. For this reason, it seems that pidgins cannot provide us with any evidence about the origin and development of natural languages; at least, the contention that they might do so has thus far not been argued conclusively:

> Returning to the main point, good reasons need to be given why it is proper to draw conclusions about facets of language evolution from data about properties of pidgins. This has not yet been attempted in explicit terms in the literature that portrays pidgins as an actual or a potential window on language evolution. (Botha 2006:12)

4.2 The written language bias in contemporary linguistics

Linell (2005) observes that there is a written language bias (WLB) in linguistics, and that a significant part of research in contemporary linguistics is strongly biased by the specific properties of written languages. His argument is that many modern conceptions of grammatical structure draw on the characteristics and properties of written languages and do not necessarily extend naturally to a proper description of spoken or signed languages, the primary goal of linguistic description.

The primacy of spoken languages is generally assumed as one of the major tenets of contemporary linguistics (Linell 2005: 28–29), as expressed by Lieberman: ‘Speech is the medium of human language. Written systems are a recent invention’ (Lieberman 2006: 59). This indeed is the standard view in current linguistics handbooks: ‘As for written languages, they too have many fascinating features, but they are regarded as *secondary* to spoken languages’ (Radford *et al.* 1999: 27).

Nevertheless, the reliability of this statement clearly depends on the interpretation of *secondary*. One of the received and generally accepted ideas of how *secondary* must be understood was formulated by Sapir thus:

> Each element (letter or written word) in the system corresponds to a specific element (sound or sound-group or spoken word) in the primary system. Written language is thus a point-to-point equivalence,

> to borrow a mathematical phrase, to its spoken counterpart. (Sapir 1921: 19–20)

However, Linell rejects this view: 'it is *not* true that written language is simply secondary to spoken language' (Linell 2005: 26). The idea of the existence of a direct correspondence between speech and writing is, according to Linell, a belief and an ideology of Western civilization (Linell 2005: 26–27). In fact, modern research in linguistics has shown repeatedly that written and spoken language differ in significant ways and that the view that written languages can be characterized as simple transcriptions of spoken languages is essentially wrong (Harris 1995, 2000; Pettersson 1996).

Nevertheless, Linell maintains that WLB is pervasive in contemporary linguistic research. If he is right, something terribly wrong is going on in today's linguistics, since what linguists are actually studying is not what they profess to analyse, that is, natural languages as acquired by children (I-Languages), but artificial versions of them, namely, the written languages that are not naturally acquired by children and must be taught at school, with differing degrees of success (E-Languages). Coulmas (1996: 455) proposes the term *scriptism* to refer to this situation, defining it as a tendency to analyse languages using (what he calls) writing-induced concepts as *phoneme*, *word*, *literal meaning* and *sentence*, while at the same time subscribing to the principle of the primacy of speech for linguistic inquiry.

This situation also has important consequences in the field of empirical linguistics. The arbitrary mixing of written and spontaneous spoken languages is very common in comparative and typologically-oriented linguistic descriptions and can lead to a serious descriptive imbalance. The problem originates when languages that do have a written form and a standard are included in a typological study (the problem almost always occurs in typological studies). Most of the grammars of these languages (mainly European or of European origin) describe some written or standard form of them, artificially elaborated at many points by the conventions of writing and by a grammatical normalization and the characteristics of the so-called educated or literary language, what we call here a cultivated and therefore artificial language, an E-Language. As a consequence, many typological surveys handle data from highly heterogeneous sources. On the one hand, we find data taken from the standardized or written version of some languages, and, on the other hand, we find data from informal everyday dialectal or idiolectal speech of languages lacking a written or standard version. This situation is in many cases more or less unavoidable:

> Typology must take account of the differences between spoken and written language. [...] While individual typologists know a

> number of languages, possibly even a large number, constraints on time and funding oblige them to draw data from grammars, and it is easy to overlook the fact that grammars of languages with written varieties will typically be based on written texts, whereas grammars of languages that have no written variety perforce describe the structure of a spoken variety. (Miller and Weinert 1998: 338)

Yet these circumstances should not lead researchers into taking some of the characteristics of informal speech and of formal written speech as a sound foundation for the proposal of typological parameters. A possible consequence of this misunderstanding would be that some of the characteristics of informal speech and of formal written speech are assigned to certain languages as typologically significant when in fact they are not.

Another important drawback of this situation arises when trying to state typological generalizations concerning the geographical distribution of grammatical patterns. This is most evident in the recent *The World's Atlas of Language Structures* (WALS).[2] In it a section is devoted to the distribution of relativization strategies in the languages of the world (Comrie and Kuteva 2005). Four main relativization strategies are distinguished, three of which will be discussed briefly here:

- The relative pronoun strategy: the position relativized is indicated inside the relative clause by means of a clause initial pronominal element, and this pronominal element is case marked (by case or by adposition) to indicate the role of the head noun within the relative clause. Example: *the lawyer from whom we received the assurances.*[3]
- The pronoun-retention strategy: the position relativized is explicitly indicated by means of a resumptive personal pronoun.
- The gap strategy: there is no overt case-marked reference to the head noun within the relative clause.

In WALS, English is assigned the first relativization strategy with respect to both the subject (Map 122[4]) and oblique (Map 123[5]) syntactic positions. This is absolutely right if we only consider standard written English:

> What then is the English relative clause typologically? We must first recognize that the term 'English relative clause' is merely a label for a set of constructions with the same function. We must also recognize that the English variant of the classical Indo-European relative clause construction belongs to written English. (This is not to deny that it occurs in speech; it occurs in planned formal spoken texts such as lectures, sermons, political speeches, and

> in the unplanned speech of highly educated people.) (Miller and Weinert 1998: 351)

But in spontaneous spoken English,[6] the pronoun-retention strategy is also found. The following examples are taken from Scottish English conversations (Miller and Weinert 1998: 347):

> *The girl that her eighteenth birthday was on that day was stoned, couldn't stand up*
> *Would those men I call their names step forward*
> *The spikes that you stick in the ground and throw rings over them.*
> *An address which I hadn't stayed there for several years.*

In the first sentence the expression *her eighteenth birthday* is used instead of the standard *whose eighteenth birthday*, in which the relative pronoun *whose* appears. In the second sentence, the expression *I call their names* would be *whose names I call* in standard written English. In the third sentence, the colloquial relative clause *throw rings over them* contrasts with the educated form *throw rings over* or *over which you throw rings*. Finally, in the fourth sentence a locative pronoun *there* indicates the role of the relative clause head (*address*). Miller and Weinert state the following about these sentences:

> They are regular constructions in non-standard English, but also occur regularly in the spontaneous speech of educated speakers. Like many other constructions in non-standard English, they are not new but can be traced back to Middle English: *the Oxford English Dictionary* has *that same cock that Peter heard him crow*. (Miller and Weinert 1998: 347)

The gap strategy can also be found in spontaneous spoken English. The following examples appear in a corpus of Scottish English conversation (Miller and Weinert 1998: 347):

> We had this French girl come to stay
> My friend's got a brother used to be in the school
> There's a man in our street has a Jaguar

In these sentences, no relative pronoun appears; if it did, as in the corresponding standard sentences (*we had this French girl who came to stay*, *my friend's got a brother who used to be in the school*, *there's a man in our street who has a Jaguar*) it would function as the subject of the relative clause. This means that the gap strategy also occurs in colloquial English in the subject position. These phenomena of colloquial English are not considered in

WALS, although they have great significance for the study of the world distribution of typological parameters:

> In spontaneous spoken English and in non-standard English the typical relative constructions is like the Persian or Semitic constructions, with an invariant complementizer. The clause following the complementizer may be like the Tamil construction in lacking a noun phrase that would occur were the clause a main clause, or it may be like the Persian and Semitic constructions in having a shadow pronoun. (Miller and Weinert 1998: 351)

To take the example of another language, Georgian is also assigned the relative clause strategy in both the subject (Map 122[7]) and oblique (Map 123[8]). But, as with English, this only applies to standard written Georgian. In colloquial Georgian things are entirely different:

> By far the most widespread clausal-relative construction in the spoken language, disposes of the above-pronouns (case-marked in order to signal overtly the function of the head-noun within the clause), in favor of the invariant, all-purpose complementiser-subordinator *rom* 'that'. […] It is possible for a pronominal copy, consisting of the demonstrative or anaphoric pronoun, to appear in the appropriate case within the clause where the head-noun is functioning as indirect object and, with certain exceptions, obligatory for this copy (followed by a postposition where necessary) to appear for positions on the hierarchy below that of indirect object. (Hewitt 1987: 187–188)

The classification of Georgian with respect to these relativization strategies is only valid for written Georgian and formal spoken Georgian. But this strategy, Hewitt claims, is not the most used in this language. Such a situation does not appear to be a singularity of English and Georgian, of course, and this same problem might arise with any other language included in WALS.

Such a clear imbalance in typological research derives from the fact that the formal written forms of some languages are compared with the colloquial spoken form of other languages (those lacking a written standard) and this comparison results in identifying the wrong typological distribution of grammatical patterns. Since all written living languages also have spontaneous spoken versions, a solution to the problem would be very straight forward. All we have to do is to compare data taken from the spontaneous spoken varieties of all the languages in a sample. That is, we would need to drop the generally assumed requirement of focusing on the standard written version of the languages in a typological comparison, and take instead data from a particular spoken dialect or idiolect of those languages, as we usually do in the case of non-standardized languages.

The central issue in comparing written discourses of some languages with colloquial discourses of other, unwritten languages is that many of the general characteristics of colloquial speech are used to characterize the grammar of languages lacking a written tradition. However, these characteristics are also present in the colloquial discourses of languages having a long written tradition. To illustrate this, let us consider the following characterization of the aboriginal Australian language Ngandi:

> Like many other Australian languages, Ngandi presents a type of discourse structure which seems to a westerner to be highly fragmented and unpredictable. Often a linguist cannot easily decide where to posit clause boundaries or even how many clauses to recognize in a given textual segment. (Heath 1985: 107)

Heath provides an analysis in his paper the following Ngandi text[9]:

ba-na'-madak	*bargu-dawal-maki-j-i*	
3PL-still-sing ritual song	3PlCLS-country-name-Neg-Fut	
gu-yaku, giyang	*bargu-mili'-dulu-bidic-ma-yi*	
CLS-absent think(ing)	3PLCLS-lest-ritual-err-Aux-Evit	
ba-ga'-yima-na-'	*angacba*	
3Pl-Sub-Durative-do that-Present-Augment		whereas
gu-ni'-yung,	*gu-dulu-wara'wara*	*gu-ga-yu-da*
CLS-this-Augment-Abs	CLS-ritual-easy	CLS-Sub-lie down-Present
gu-yimin'-yung,	*dawal-mayin-gu-yung*	
CLS-thing-Abs	country-naming-Gen-Abs	

> '...they (old men) still sing the ritual, (but) they cannot call out the country names, not at all, thinking they might err, they (think) that way, but actually this, this is an easy ritual it is (lying down), the thing, about naming countries.'

As Heath says, the English translation suggests a clumsy, groping style that is normal in Ngandi texts. This author observes that there are pauses between constituents belonging to a single clause and two juxtaposed distinct clauses (*guduluwara'wara* and *gugayuda*) with no conjunction at all. In the last part of the text it can also be seen that there is some sort of reformulation of the subject under discussion, which is rephrased as 'the thing, about naming the countries', as if the speaker was having difficulty choosing the proper expression. The author adds that this is frequently the case in Ngandi discourse (Heath 1985: 102). He arrives at the following conclusion:

> We have seen, then, that the surface syntactic structure is formally problematic. Frequent incursive pauses give the syntax a choppy, fragmented character in which various constituents have little or no obvious surface relationships to each other (fixed order, fixed types of intonational contour, etc.). On the other hand, two clauses (or two clause kernels each containing a predicate) may be run together in a single breath. (Heath 1985: 103)

Following these comments, Heath assigns these typical features of colloquial speech to the Ngandi language in general, and goes on to compare this characterization of the Ngandi language with English:

> It is presumptuous to view these simply as low-level performance features overlaid on a more crystalline deep structure with clear clause boundaries. Fragmentation of surface structure is a basic feature of Ngandi which differentiates it from English and many other languages (including free-word-order languages with sharp clause boundaries). (Heath 1985: 103)

These comments are based on the idea that English clause structure, in contrast to that of Ngandi, is well defined and coherent. But such a comparison is correct only if we consider formal, written English. Colloquial English is a great deal closer to colloquial Ngandi with respect to syntactic fragmentation. Consider, for example, the following extract of colloquial English discourse:[10]

> no if we can get Louise/ I mean her mother and father/ Louise's parents would give us / they've got a big car and keep the mini for the week// but Louise isnae too keen on the idea so …

Miller and Weinert (1998: 60) give the following formal, written version of the same extract:

> No. Louise's parents have got a big car. If we can get them to give us the big car and if they would take the Mini for the week [we could travel by car together]. But Louise is not too keen on the idea, so [we will not be travelling in the big car].

In the written version we have a complete and coherent syntax and the information is well organized and presented in a logical, incremental way. The corresponding colloquial discourse seems to be highly fragmented and elliptical with poor syntax and semantics, and showing chaotic organization.

Compared with this text, the Ngandi discourse presented earlier seems much more coherent and meaningful.

Miller and Weinert (1998) make the following comment on the usability and efficacy of this kind of real, colloquial English discourse:

> From a comparison of the written and spoken versions it is only too easy to conclude that the spoken text is a hopeless piece of communication with fragmented and incomplete syntax and a badly organized sequence of information. The fact is that none of the participants in the conversation appeared to notice anything amiss, the field-worker did not hesitate or ask the speaker for clarification and the conversation continued smoothly. Even more interestingly, groups of students who have been asked to listen to the section of the conversation containing [the text] have also failed to notice the syntactic problems until they saw the transcription and were asked to analyse its syntax. (Miller and Weinert 1998: 60)

We know that spontaneous colloquial language, based on our natural I-Language competence, precedes both ontogenetically and phylogenetically the formal written language, and that this formal written language is a culturally determined artificial elaboration of an E-language. For this reason, we can view the formal written English text as a more or less artificial linguistic elaboration of the spoken text, but not the other way around. It makes no sense, in modern linguistics terms, to conceive of the colloquial text as a defective and poor instantiation of the written text. Colloquial English is not a defective version of formal written English. Natural I-Language competence is not a poor or defective implementation of the grammatical competence which those in industrialized societies typically acquired at school.

Some conclusions can be drawn from the preceding observations. First, the apparently fragmented and incoherent syntax of colloquial discourse does not prove that the corresponding language lacks grammatical rules and principles. All English and Ngandi syntax (colloquial or otherwise) is produced on the basis of grammatical rules and syntactic principles. Second, all colloquial texts can be subjected to a process of elaboration according to the artificial principles of a cultivated language; this can be made with English colloquial texts but also with Ngandi colloquial texts: the fact that there is no formal written Ngandi does not mean that such an elaborated language could not be produced if the requirement arose. Indeed, as we have already noted, aboriginal languages are elaborated in order to obtain specific cultivated versions. Third, and in anticipation of the following chapter, it should be emphasized that we cannot draw any conclusions about the simplicity or complexity of two or more languages by comparing spontaneous colloquial texts from some of them with formal written texts from others. This procedure is epistemologically and empirically mistaken and can lead to flawed conclusions, especially if we also fail to make the distinction between natural and cultivated languages.

Notes

1. For a detailed explanation of literary elaboration of natural languages see Fabb (1997, 2002), on which the rest of this section is based.
2. Haspelmath, Dryer, Gil and Comrie, eds. (2005)
3. This example is borrowed from Miller and Weinert (1998: 346), Comrie and Kuteva (2005: 494) give a German sentence to exemplify this strategy.
4. Comrie and Kuteva (2005: 498).
5. Comrie and Kuteva (2005: 500).
6. For a useful survey of relative clause formation in non-standard European varieties, see Murelli (2011).
7. Comrie and Kuteva (2005: 498).
8. Comrie and Kuteva (2005: 500).
9. This text is taken from Heath (1985: 101). Some of the diacritics and abbreviations have been slightly changed or omitted. The following abbreviations are used: 3Pl = third person plural, CLS = classifier affix, Neg = negation, Fut = future, Aux= auxiliar, Evit = evitative affix, Sub = subordinator, Gen = genitive, Abs = absolute.
10. Taken from a corpus of spontaneous conversation (Miller and Weinert 1998: 60)

5 The mismeasure of language diversity

The second chapter of this book set out a naturalistic view of human language entailing the hypothesis of the uniformity of languages. However, it is not uncommon in current literature to find attitudes and opinions that challenge such a hypothesis. We have already briefly discussed some of them, criticizing the inadequacy of the notion of language change that seems to underline such views. In the current chapter we will consider in more detail how the confusion between the natural and cultural dimensions of language has led to what are, in our opinion, erroneous positions favouring a revival of linguistic relativism.

5.1 The false problem of natural language complexity

As discussed in section 3.3, the assumption that all natural languages present a similar degree of complexity has been considered as one the pillars of contemporary linguistics. The assumption arises from the following empirically observable facts:

- All humans share exactly the same physical and cognitive constraints, abilities and predispositions.
- All human beings can acquire any natural human language in a spontaneous way.
- Language structure is independent of the social, economical or political development of human societies.

With respect to the first item, Fitch (echoing Chomsky) notes the following incontrovertible fact:

> The simple fact that a dog or a cat or a chimpanzee raised in a human home will not acquire language, while a human child will, indicates the existence of *some* biological basis in our species. (Fitch 2010: 81)[1]

The second item is formulated by Fitch as follows:

> A core fact of human nature is that any normal human can learn any of the 6,000 or so natural languages currently existing, if raised from birth in an environment where that language is used. (Fitch 2010: 27)

These two ideas must be taken together, not separately:

> One could easily choose either the biological preparedness present in all normal children, or the great variety of languages a child can handle, as an interesting focus for a lifetime of research. Unfortunately, a tendency to focus exclusively on one or the other has generated one of the most persistently fruitless debates in science: the 'nature *versus* nurture' debate. (Fitch 2010: 27)

In relation to the second item, one of the earliest statements on the independence between culture and language is attributed to F. Schlegel by Darwin:

> Thus F. Schlegel writes: 'In those languages which appear to be at the lowest grade of intellectual culture, we frequently observe a very high and elaborate degree of art in their grammatical structure. This is especially the case with the Basque and the Lapponian, and many of the American languages.' (Darwin 1871: 114)[2]

In his introduction to the study of speech Sapir was particularly clear with respect to the question of the association between language and the development of culture:

> From this it follows that all attempts to connect particular types of linguistic morphology with certain correlated stages of cultural development are vain. Rightly understood, such correlations are rubbish. The merest *coup d'oeil* verifies our theoretical argument on this point. Both simple and complex types of language of an indefinite number of varieties may be found spoken at any desired level of cultural advance. When it comes to linguistic form, Plato walks with the Macedonian swineherd, Confucius with the head hunting savage of Assam. (Sapir 1922: 219)

Recent theoretical developments in linguistic analysis confirm that Sapir was indeed correct in his position here:

> The grammar of a group's language does not seem to be correlated with other identifiable features of their culture. As we look at how the different language types are distributed around the world, there is no hint of a significant interaction between language type and cultural type. Japanese, Mongolian, Malayalam, Turkish, Basque, Amharic, Greenlandic Eskimo, Siouan, Choctaw,

> Diegeño, Quechua, and New Guinean languages are all head-final languages. Chinese, Thai, Indonesian, Arabic, Russian, French, Yoruba, Swahili, Salish, Zapotec, Mayan, and Waurá are all head-initial languages. Is there anything in the pattern of cultural interactions or the basic world view of the first group of people that consistently distinguishes them from the second group? Is there any causal relationship between how they order their words and how they experience life? So far as anyone knows, the answer is no. (Baker 2001: 201)

In addition, this phenomenon can be taken as evidence in favour of a universal linguistic basis for language, as expressed by Nevins *et al.*:

> If speakers acquire the same types of languages whether their home is a German city, a village in the Caucasus, or the banks of the Maici River in Amazonas, Brazil, we have discovered just the kind of disassociation between language and culture that sheds light on the nature and structure of UG. (Nevins *et al.* 2009: 359)

All these ideas make sense when we speak about natural languages. But they clearly do not apply to cultivated languages. Depending of the degree of elaboration exerted on a natural language, a cultivated language can be more or less complex. Certainly, written Sanskrit, Classical Arabic or Classical Latin are complex and difficult languages; it is not easy to master them, in that they were created through a systematic elaboration of a natural language. But these are not natural languages, but rather cultivated languages; they are highly culture dependent and cannot be acquired spontaneously and used freely and effortlessly. Classical Arabic must be studied by children at school, but no human being is equipped to naturally assimilate such a language. This is because these languages are not in fact natural languages. In order to assess the linguistic degree of complexity we cannot, of course, compare a natural language with a cultivated language, yet this flawed method is indeed used when, for example, written Standard English is compared with informal spoken Indonesian to assess differences in complexity (see below). In light of our discussion here, such an approach is clearly wrong, and will lead to distorted results. Rather, the comparison ought to be between informal spontaneous (or dialectal) English and informal spontaneous (or dialectal) Indonesian; or to compare written Standard English with written Standard Indonesian.

In order to determine the degree of language complexity it is necessary to explore this concept in more detail. Gell-Mann (1994) examined the issue in the opening chapters of his book on complexity. First, he speaks about the subjectivity of the concept of complexity:

> If complexity is defined in terms of the length of a description, then it is not an intrinsic property of the thing described. Obviously, the length of a description may depend on who or what is doing the describing. [...] Any definition of complexity is necessarily context-dependent, even subjective. Of course, the level of detail at which the system is being described is already somewhat subjective – it too depends on the observer or the observing equipment. In actuality, then, we are discussing one or more definitions of complexity that depend on a description of one system by another system, presumably a complex adaptive system, which could be a human observer. Suppose, for present purposes, that the describing system is, in fact, a human observer. (Gell-Mann 1994: 33)

The same idea has been proposed by Kusters in his study of the complexity of verbal inflection:

> The moral of this story is that there is no way to define complexity without being specific about to **whom** a language is or is not complex. In other words, complexity is not a simple predicate attributable to language but a relation between two entities: a language and someone who evaluates the language. (Kusters 2003: 6)

In light of the assumptions of contemporary linguistic theory, any discussion of linguistic complexity must begin with the idea that the grammars of all natural languages exist as particular combinations of the same basic constituent units and principles:

> It is a common observation that for all their diversity, languages are made to a great extent of familiar pieces, much like the wide variety of shapes and objects that can be assembled from a limited array of Lego blocks. This general characterization of the constrained nature of linguistic variation is consistent with a variety of theories about the nature of the building blocks and the ways in which they may be combined in particular languages. Nonetheless, it still characterizes well the practical experience of linguists who encounter the data of an unfamiliar language. It is this context that makes it meaningful to describe languages by typologically characterizing their properties ('head-final', 'WH-in-situ', etc.) and to use standard names for these properties, even when describing unfamiliar languages. (Nevins *et al.* 2009: 359)

The natural phenomenon of universal language acquisition – any human child can naturally acquire any human language – also argues in favour of the view that there is a profound unity between all human natural languages:

> The expectations children bring to language learning must be substantial enough to help them master the complexities of language with relative ease yet general enough to be applicable to any human language they come into contact with. This implies that all human languages must be more similar than they appear. Since all are equally within the grasp of a healthy human child to learn through ordinary, informal exposure, they must, with all their distinguishing intricacies, be fundamentally commensurable. This conceptual argument from language learning, even more than the phenomenon of intertranslatability, convinces linguists that at some level all languages must be the same. (Baker 2001:14)

Let us take a specific example of the subjective components of a grammarian's definition of complexity as referred to by Gell-Mann. Complex morphology is one of the main criteria used for estimating the overall complexity of a language; specifically, 'inflectional morphology renders a grammar more complex than another one in most cases' (McWhorter 2001: 137). This seems to be a fairly objective criterion for estimating grammatical complexity; yet in reality it is not. A great deal of subjectivity is involved, as Gell-Mann notes. Basque verbal morphology offers an interesting case in point. Thus, both Basque and Georgian verbal morphologies are usually considered as extremely complex:

> As in Georgian, a relatively simple nominal system is accompanied by a very complicated verbal system. But whereas in Georgian the complication lies in the proliferation of permutations and combinations to which the sense-verb is subjected, in Basque the sense-verb itself usually appears in simple stem or participial form, accompanied by an enormously rich network of auxiliary forms which are deictically coded for person and regimen, and which are quasi-bound in the sense that they only acquire full meaning when associated with a sense-verb stem. For example, by itself *diot* indicates action by first person singular directed in some way at third person singular, i.e. specifies a deictic relationship. (Campbell 1991: 180)

This description of Basque verbal morphology contains the expression 'enormously rich network of auxiliary forms', a phrase that might induce in the reader an impression of bewildering complexity completely alien to the more common patterns of other European languages such as English, German or French. Indeed, some descriptions of Basque verbal morphology could easily confirm and reinforce this impression. The classical Basque grammar by Ithurry (1895), for example, runs to 453 pages, with the description of verbal morphology occupying 351 of these (from page 57 to page 408) and containing more than 260 conjugation tables with little or no explanation. This form of describing the verbal morphology of Basque can lead to the impression that the language is extraordinarily complex and that learning Basque is beyond the capabilities of most mortals. Yet we know that this cannot be true; children acquire the particular dialect described by Ithurry spontaneously without experiencing any exceptional difficulties. We also know that adults speak it as fluently and automatically as the speakers of other apparently simpler natural languages.

In his empirical study on the complexity of verbal inflection in Arabic, Scandinavian, Quechua and Swahili, Kusters is very clear on this point:

> An L1 learner has no problems with inflectional categories, and even prefers them above other devices. A symbolic user may exploit inflectional categories for reasons of verbal culture or identity shaping. (Kusters 2003: 51)

Kusters here refers to the fact that inflectional categories are learnable as part of the process of natural language acquisition. He also makes another important point in noting that inflectional categories can be subjected to elaboration in linguistic social cultivation: the expression *symbolic user* refers precisely to this type of intentional language modification.

Modern, scientific descriptions of Basque verbal morphology offer a wholly different picture. In their excellent grammar of Basque, framed within modern linguistic criteria, Hualde, Oyharçabal and Ortiz de Urbina give a comprehensive description of Basque verbal morphology in only 47 pages (Hualde and Ortiz de Urbina, 2003: 195–242), including just 75 conjugation tables.[3] In another comprehensive descriptive Basque grammar, this time written in Basque, we find only 58 conjugation tables (Zubiri 2000: 405–600). These conjugations conform to only two general conjugation models (that of the auxiliaries corresponding to *to be* and *to have*) containing three versions for the intransitive auxiliary (with and without an indirect object and an allocutive version) and three for the transitive auxiliary (with and without an indirect object and an allocutive form), and by the synthetic conjugations of 20 verbs (also with three versions) that follow the same conjugation pattern. In sum, there are only nine conjugational models in Basque (that include present and past forms in the indicative and subjunctive modes) and only two irregular verbs (the two auxiliaries). The Basque verbal system is clearly not a simple one, but is essentially no more complex than those of other languages such as Spanish or French.

Generally, considerations as to the complexity of a language are based on a superficial analysis of language structure in two related senses. First, they focus on immediately visible linguistic components (number of phonemes, number of cases, number of inflectional forms …). The following observations by Moro on the verbal complexity of English and Italian are enlightening here, and merit extensive quotation:

> Languages that seem easy in some aspects are more difficult in others. For example, verbal morphology (the forms that the verbs can take) is certainly easier in English than it is in Italian. Aside from a few irregular verbs, English verbal morphology is minimal, making a change in the spelling of a verb in the third-person singular present, the past tense, in passive and the progressive forms. [...] Italian, by contrast, has an extremely rich verbal morphology that distinguishes person, number, tense, mood, and so on. [...] In some respects, however, the syntax of English is more complex than Italian. For instance, the subject *John* and the verb *arrives* can be combined only into the string *John arrives* and not **Arrives John*. In Italian, both *Gianni arriva* and *arriva Gianni* are correct. If we assume that syntax is a set of filters that eliminate impossible combinations, we have to conclude that English has one more filter in its syntax according to which the subject cannot follow the verb in declarative sentences, thus the syntax is more complex in this respect. It is important to repeat the idea that until we have an explicit matrix to measure the complexity of different languages, we will have to settle for limited evaluations such as the one above. The most plausible conclusion, however, is still that languages do not differ in *global* complexity. (Moro 2008: 112–113, author's italics).

The second sense is that such considerations of complexity often neglect hidden or covert linguistic properties that can only be exposed by a sophisticated linguistic analysis. Bisang (2009) has noted the issue of such hidden properties in his discussion of the grammar of Thai and Chinese, convincingly showing that superficial or self-evident grammatical complexity is not a sound basis for a treatment of complexity:

> [C]omplexity is not just a matter of looking at surface phenomena like word order rules or the presence of obligatory and overt grammatical markers. The existence of different analyses of one and the same surface structure adds a considerable degree of hidden complexity to a language. In the case of East and mainland Southeast Asian languages, this type of structural complexity is considerably higher than a language like English because many markers that are associated with a given construction are not obligatory. Thus, the absence of a marker does not exclude the presence of the construction it is related to. (Bisang 2009: 43)

The superficial analysis of linguistic data as a means of inferring the complexity of a language, as criticized by Bisang, is perfectly illustrated by Gil (2009), who examines the following simple sentence of Riau Indonesian:

> Riau Indonesian (Gil 2009: 23)
> *Ayam* *makan*
> chicken eat

According to Gil, this sentence 'consists entirely of two "content words", and is devoid of any additional grammatical markers' (Gil 2009: 23), and for him the sentence illustrates the fact that the language is highly associational. He explains this linguistic feature in the following way:

> The *associational* character of the language can be seen in the wide range of available interpretations: the first word, *ayam*, is underspecified for number and definiteness; the second word, *makan*, is indeterminate with respect to tense and aspect; and the sentence as a whole is underspecified with regard to thematic roles, with *ayam* being able to bear agent, patient, or any other relation to *makan*, and in addition also indeterminate with respect to ontological categories, with possible interpretation belonging to categories such as activity, thing, reason, place, time and others. (Gil 2009: 23)

If this is indeed an adequate analysis of the Riau Indonesian sentence, then it could be interpreted as 'The chicken is eating', 'The chickens that were eaten' or 'The reason chickens eat' among other possible meanings (Gil 2009: 23), and thus it can safely be said that this language presents an extreme degree of covert or hidden complexity.[4] Such a conclusion is unavoidable, since we have to suppose that when Riau Indonesian speakers use this sentence, in a particular context, they construct a unique intended grammatical interpretation that can be perfectly identified by the hearer: this interpretation must be based on formal (although non-audible) grammatical properties, guaranteeing an adequate grammatical analysis on the part of the addressee. If sentence interpretation in Riau Indonesian were not based on hidden grammatical structuring, we would expect non-uniformity in the sense that, in general, Riau Indonesian addressees would not be able to determine in a uniform way the intended meaning of a linguistic expression in a particular context. Gil does not report any difficulties by native speakers of Riau Indonesian in determining the intended meaning of sentences in particular contexts, and maintains that in Riau Indonesian 'simple forms map onto simple meanings with no reason to believe that the pragmatics then automatically steps in to fill in any number of additional more complex details' (Gil 2009: 24). Despite such an (unproved) assumption, it is clear that without a formal grammatical structuring of Riau Indonesian expressions, this mapping would be utterly hopeless since, as Gil himself observes, each sentence could be interpreted in many different ways, and therefore, could be associated with many different meanings.

Clearly, Gil's analysis is based on purely superficial observations and not on a deep syntactic analysis of Riau Indonesian sentences; yet a deep syntactic analysis is needed, since it is the only factor that could account for the efficient use of this language in everyday life, assuming that its users communicate with each other automatically and without ostensible difficulties in their day-to-day lives. Without a formal determination of the intended interpretation of apparently ambiguous sentences in Riau Indonesian, this phenomenon is impossible to account for on a rational basis. Surely, then, there is a great deal more to the syntax of Riau Indonesian sentences than Gil's analysis assumes, and a description of this hidden syntax requires a more sophisticated theory of grammatical description that the one used by Gil.[5]

Nominal case inflection offers a good illustration of the important difference between a superficial, morphological based approach to language complexity and an approach recognizing hidden or covert complexity, the latter more in tune with the theoretical developments of contemporary linguistics. The number of inflectional nominal cases can be used to arrive at a classification of grammatical complexity. In this classification, languages like Chinese, Vietnamese and Indonesian, lacking morphological case endings, would be the simplest languages, whereas Finnish, Hungarian and Basque, with more than ten nominal case endings, would be considered the most complex; languages such as Latin, German, Korean, Japanese and Turkish, with less than ten, would lie somewhere between the two extremes.

Yet the simple inventory and study of the use of morphological case endings barely scratches the surface of the extremely complex morphosyntactic phenomenon of case assignment. In order to embrace this grammatical feature more fully, Case Theory can be of some assistance. In the hidden complexity involved in case assignment, it is crucial to distinguish between morphological and abstract case, noted as Case in this theory. Many languages do not have morphological case distinction, but this does not mean that distinctions of case are not operative at a syntactic level:

> Nevertheless this does not mean that the notion of Case is redundant for languages without morphological Case distinctions, as Case plays an important role in many languages in determining the distributions of DPs, not just the form of nominals. [...] We therefore need a more general notion of Case distinct from the traditional notion of nominal morphological form, to be called abstract Case (as opposed to morphological case). Abstract Case

> is a property which is borne by a nominal element as a result of occupying certain positions. (Cook and Newson 2007: 147)

Abstract case assignment is very important for describing different and apparently unrelated syntactic phenomena.[6] For example, in order to analyse the syntax of an English sentence like *John seems to like Mary*, where *John* functions as the deep subject of *like*, it is necessary to resort to the notion of Case. The proper noun *John* appears as the surface subject of *seem* (despite the fact that John does not 'seem' anything) because *to like* cannot assign abstract case to it. This same constraint is also responsible for the position of patient-denoting subjects in passive sentences such as *John was interrogated* (see Cook and Newson 2007: 159–160).

As a consequence, in order to measure properly the grammatical complexity of grammars with respect to case marking it would be necessary to take into account all the hidden or covert details involved in such a phenomenon, some of which may be poorly understood, or might even have gone unnoticed thus far. A mere inspection of the superficial morphological manifestation of case in different languages tells us relatively little about their grammatical structures, and hence is not a credible point of departure for assessing grammatical complexity, let alone linguistic complexity.

Many times, the complexity of written grammars depends on the language in which another language's grammar is described. If the two languages are closely related to each other, the grammatical description of that language will not be especially complicated. But if the language we wish to describe grammatically differs in many respects from the language which serves as a departure point, the grammatical description will surely be much more large and complex.

The mere formulation of McWorther's first assumption on the assessment of grammatical complexity is a clear example of this type of bias:

> The normal state of language is highly complex, to an extent that seems extreme to speakers of languages like English. (McWorther 2011: 1)[7]

Gell-Mann warns us about the idea of measuring grammatical complexity by the size of a grammatical description:

> One may think of grammatical complexity in terms of a textbook of grammar. Roughly speaking, the longer the textbook, the more complex the grammar. This agrees very well with the notion of complexity as the length of a schema. Every nasty little exception adds to the length of the book and the grammatical complexity of the language. (Gell-Mann 1994: 55)

This approach can lead us into superficial and biased conclusions:

> As to the level of initial knowledge, consider an old-fashioned grammar of a foreign language written in English for English speakers. It will not have to introduce so many new grammatical ideas to the reader if it is a grammar of Dutch (fairly similar to English and closely related) rather than of Navajo, which is very different from English in structure. The grammar of Navajo should be longer. Similarly, a hypothetical grammar of Dutch written for speakers of Navajo would presumably have to be longer than a grammar of Dutch written for English speakers. (Gell-Mann 1994: 55)

An empirical description of the I-language, the grammatical competence of the speakers as it is, would be much more advisable:

> Even taking these factors into account, it is still reasonable to relate the grammatical complexity of a language to the length of a textbook describing its grammar. However, it would be more interesting if it were possible instead to look inside the brain of a native speaker (as advancing technology may some day make possible) and see how the grammar is encoded there. The length of the schema represented by that internal grammar would provide a somewhat less arbitrary measure of grammatical complexity. (Naturally, the definition of length in this case may be a subtle one, depending on how the bits of grammatical information are actually encoded. Are they inscribed locally in neurons and synapses or distributed somehow over a whole network?) (Gell-Mann 1994: 55–56)

It is therefore crucial to distinguish between effective complexity with respect to an observer and internal absolute complexity, in Gell-Mann's terms:

> We define the effective complexity of an entity, relative to a complex adaptive system that is observing it and constructing a schema, as the length of a concise description of the entity's regularities identified in the schema. We can use the term 'internal effective complexity' when the schema somehow governs the system under discussion (as grammar stored in the brain regulates speech), rather than merely being used by an external observer, such as the author of a grammatical text. (Gell-Mann 1994: 56)

In order to assess the statements about language complexity found in the linguistic literature, it is very important not to confuse cultivated and natural languages. As we have seen, cultivated languages result from intentional elaborations of some aspects of the natural languages on which they are based (E-languages). This means that, compared with natural languages, cultivated languages can be much more complex in certain dimensions. But the important thing to bear in mind is that cultivated languages are not natural languages, as E-languages have a completely different status, and therefore, cannot be compared with them in order to assess natural language complexity.

Maas (2009) has made exactly this point:

> Things become more complicated when grammar has to cope with literate tasks. In doing so, it has to exploit the resources of the available linguistic structures – which can mean different things in languages such as Mongolian and English. And of course, all this is overlaid by non-functional, but often rigid, normative patterns established in the relevant culture and, in some cases, foreign models used as sparring partners in elaborating literate structures. (Maas 2009: 177)

As we have seen, this means that we cannot compare, for example, standard written English with spontaneous spoken Haitian in order to determine the grammatical complexity of these languages. We are comparing highly disparate entities: a cultivated language and a natural language. We know that this problem can easily be overcome if we take spontaneous oral English for the purpose of such a comparison, thus allowing us to compare two natural languages. It has been demonstrated beyond doubt that the grammar of spontaneous spoken English differs in many details from that of written Standard English (Miller and Weinert 1998) and that in many respects some of the syntactic complexities that can be found in formal written English are absent in the spontaneous language. For example, concerning formal written English Miller and Weinert observe the following:

> To summarize, as illustrated by the above written-language examples, NPs in written language can potentially contain any number and a large variety of pre-modifying and post-modifying elements. (Miller and Weinert 1998: 139)

Nevertheless, the possibilities observed in spontaneous spoken speech are much more restricted (Miller and Weinert 1998: 139–159). In both cases, the data come from linguistic products, i.e. E-language. Nevertheless, the differences do not always arise from performance constraints; in some cases, they involve different grammatical rules. In such cases, only data from spontaneous spoken language can serve as a means of assessing natural grammatical competence.

The superficial approach to language complexity just illustrated has to do with certain language products pertaining to E-language, not to I-language. For example, the nominal and verbal paradigms, like inflectional tables in general, are artificially elaborated products of certain aspects of the activity of natural grammatical competences. Moreover, these products are collected, organized and systematized by grammarians, with the application of specific linguistic criteria. For example, an inflectional paradigm in a written grammar collects, in an ordered way, some of the possible products of a certain grammatical competence. The patterning and structuring of those paradigms are proposed by the linguist, not by the native speaker. When linguists compare different inflectional paradigms in order to ascertain language complexity they are in fact comparing different techniques of classification used by linguists to account for a certain linguistic behaviour. Such classifications and patterns tell us something about the skills and capabilities of linguists and linguistic models, but cannot be used to assess the grammatical complexities of I-languages.

5.2 Language interbreeding

In our approach to the comparison between the evolution of species and that of languages (see 2.1.1) we have identified life with language, and the criterion of fertile breeding used in defining natural species (groups of organisms) with the criterion of similarity (based, in the absence of better metrics, on the criterion of mutual intelligibility) to define natural languages (groups of I-languages). It is clear that tiger A is closer to tiger B than to an elephant, and that the I-language of a Russian from Moscow is closer to the I-language of a Russian from St Petersburg than to the I-language of a German from Berlin. In both cases these barriers are the effect of the historical accumulation of differences.

But while we have used this equivalence to enhance the comparison, we have pointed out that in fact the segmentation between different languages is arbitrary, since the existing objects (the I-languages) form a continuum (see 2.1.2).[8] Ultimately, *Homo sapiens* represents a single linguistic species and, in this sense, all languages belong to the same linguistic species.

If we return in this context to Hauser *et al.*'s (2002) distinction between FLN and FLB, we note that such a distinction permits them to state the following hypothesis:

> On the basis of data reviewed below, we hypothesize that most, if not all, of FLB is based on mechanisms shared with nonhuman

> animals (as held by hypothesis 1). In contrast, we suggest that FLN – the computational mechanism of recursion – is recently evolved and unique to our species. (Hauser *et al.* 2002: 1573)

This means that the human language faculty has many things in common with the analogue communicative and cognitive faculties of other species and also that there is something special (but not necessarily *some thing*!), perhaps the FLN, that makes the human language faculty distinct from other animal communication systems. In other words: human languages, as manifestation of FLN, must be considered as 'linguistic organs' different from the other animal 'linguistic organs'. In addition, all cognitive systems, human and non-human, are related from an evolutionary point of view, since FLB seems to have a long evolutionary history:

> FLB as a whole thus has an ancient evolutionary history, long predating the emergence of language, and a comparative analysis is necessary to understand this complex system. By contrast, according to recent linguistic theory, the computations underlying FLN may be quite limited. [...] By this hypothesis, FLB contains a wide variety of cognitive and perceptual mechanisms shared with other species, but only those mechanisms underlying FLN – particularly its capacity for discrete infinity – are uniquely human. (Hauser *et al.* 2002: 1573)

All human natural languages are direct manifestations of the language faculty (FLB). In biological terms, this means that all human I-languages belong to the same linguistic species, if we focus on the faculty of language in the narrow sense (FLN).

As we have discussed, species are defined as groups of individuals capable of interbreeding and producing fertile offspring. If it is true that all I-languages are superficial variations of the same human faculty for language, then it is predicted that, to extend the comparison, all I-languages should be able to interbreed and produce fertile offspring. Hence, there is an even clearer analogue to the biological property of interbreeding in the linguistic sphere: language 'interbreeding' results in so-called contact and mixed languages.

When two different linguistic populations with no or little inter-comprehensibility interact in a sustained way, mixed variations of the two languages often appear in a spontaneous way. These languages are natural languages, having all the properties determined by FLN. This is not the case with non-human animal communication systems. Following Hauser, Chomsky and Fitch's proposal, we can re-state the observation that the different communication systems in the non-human animal world correspond to distinct language species. As such, the 'natural languages' that belong to different species cannot mix or 'interbreed' in order to produce new natural languages or new natural communication systems. Such a claim seems to be uncontroversial: thus far no natural language based on two or more communicative systems of two different species has been discovered. For example, the communicative systems of dolphins, birds and chimpanzees, in contact with a human language, have never given rise to a new human or non-human natural language. Of course, it is possible to teach a dolphin or a chimpanzee some sort of rudimentary sign or visual language, but these are not natural languages, since they have to be purposely instructed and are not spontaneously acquired;[9] such instructed languages, in that they are artificial, could never match the usability and subtlety of natural communication by humans, dolphins or chimpanzees, as Fitch has pointed out:

> From my perspective, Kanzi and other language-trained apes demonstrate an ability to acquire a sizeable lexicon, to use it in communicative interactions (though mostly, it must be admitted, to make requests for treats or tickles), and to produce and understand basic and non-random combinations of these lexical items. These communicative abilities do not constitute a language by the simple definition used in this book, because Kanzi cannot communicate all the concepts he can entertain. For example, Kanzi can successfully carry out quite complex motor actions, such as starting fires and making and using simple stone tools [...], but his 'linguistic' productions never even come close to the complexity required to describe these abilities. (Fitch 2010: 168)

We postulate the following axiom concerning linguistic contact:

> *As members of the same linguistic species, any two human natural languages in a contact situation can give rise to a new distinct natural language*

One of the main empirical bases demonstrating that every natural human language belongs to the same species of communicative-cognitive system can be found in the ubiquitous phenomenon of language contact. When two or more natural languages come into contact, new natural human languages can arise, no matter how different these human languages are. English is a spectacular demonstration of this;[10] in the following diagram we include some of the new natural languages originating on the basis of contact between English and other languages of the world:

English varieties coming from linguistic contact[11]

New natural language	*Contact languages (other than English)*
Krio	Portuguese, Yoruba, Arabic, French
Liberian	Portuguese, African languages
Sranan	Dutch, Portuguese
Saramaccan	Portuguese, Dutch, African languages
Ndjuka	Portuguese, Dutch, African languages
Hawaiian English	Polynesian and Asian languages
Tok Pisin	Austronesian languages
Torres Strait Creole	Australian and Papuan languages
Fanakalo	African languages

All these natural languages are said to be creoles: a special type of mixed natural language. In spite of what it is often maintained, they are not in any way deviated or exceptional natural languages compared to other natural languages, such as colloquial English, French or Spanish.

The myth of creole exceptionalism, critiqued by DeGraff (2005), is founded on the claim that these mixed languages are not in fact normal natural languages. Many creoles emerged from the very specific sociolinguistic conditions of slavery and the slave trade; but such circumstances do not affect either the FLB or the FLN, and hence these new languages developed as natural human languages. Throughout its history, humanity has known many different social and political situations, yet none of these, it seems, has affected the human language faculty in any ostensible or indeed notable way. On the contrary, such a faculty has evolved in spite of the countless vicissitudes of human history.

It is important to note that the so-called creole languages are primarily spontaneous spoken languages rather than educated written ones. This in turn means that they are natural languages, not artificial or elaborated languages, and that our reasoning in the preceding section is valid here. For instance, Haitian Creole is a natural spontaneous spoken language and in this sense it should be compared with sixteenth-century spontaneous spoken French, not with the written French of that time. For this reason it makes no sense to say that Haitian Creole is a simplification or a deviation of the standard French language (Chaudenson 2003: 138–146, 193).

Another important point needs clarification here. The idea that creoles derive from pidgins is well established in the linguistic literature. Yet the empirical evidence here is in fact poor, and following Chaudenson (2003: 50–51) we can now say with reasonable confidence that French-based creoles do not proceed from French pidgins.

Mufwene (2008: 75) observes that pidgins and creoles tend to originate in different places:

> A simple look at the geographical distribution of our heuristic prototypes of creoles and pidgins suggests already that the alleged pidgin ancestry of creoles is questionable at best. Most pidgins are concentrated on the Atlantic coast of the African mainland and on Pacific Islands, whereas most of the creoles that have evolved from European languages, the only ones that matter for our purposes, are concentrated on Atlantic and Indian Ocean islands (including places such as Cape Verde and São Tomé) and on the Atlantic coast of the Americas. (Mufwene 2008: 75)

Pidgins originate in sporadic and specific situations of language contact, giving rise to very simplified and limited contact varieties that can only be used in a few situations. They are not learned by children in a spontaneous way, but intentionally acquired by adults for certain specific purposes, such as trading. This means, as we noted above, that they are artificial or elaborated languages in which certain modifications are intentionally made in order to simplify a particular language for making communication easier.

In contrast, creoles typically develop in plantation settlement colonies in which new non-standard vernaculars of a European language can constitute the basis for an entirely new language. In this case, regular interaction occurs between speakers of European and non-European languages, creating the need to fully acquire a European language. The particular kind of development seen with creoles is not intentional – on the contrary, the speakers try to approximate as fully as possible to an (already colonial) variety of the corresponding European language – and it is completely spontaneous:

> The earliest vernaculars commonly spoken and appropriated by non-Europeans were approximations of the European colonial languages forged in part by the nonnative European indentured servants with whom the slaves interacted regularly. (Mufwene 2008: 77)

In fact, Mufwene believes that the sociolinguistic conditions in which creoles develop exclude the creation of a pidgin variety:

> [C]reoles did not develop from pidgins […] The reason is that the intimate living conditions shared by Europeans and non-Europeans alike during the homestead phase of settlement colonies made no allowance for the development of pidgins as structurally reduced language varieties associated with sporadic contacts. (Mufwene 2008: 77)

As we noted previously, creoles should be compared with spoken non-standard spontaneous European languages, not with standard European languages. Indeed, most of the grammatical features said to characterize Creole languages can also be found in the non-standard colloquial varieties of their corresponding base languages:

> Alternately, creoles' structures should be compared with those of other vernaculars that have evolved from the koinés spoken by the proletarian European settlers, the typical founder populations of European colonies, with whom non-Europeans lived fairly intimately during the homestead phase. (Mufwene 2008: 84)

Muwfene (2008: 84) lists some grammatical features shared by English creoles and non-Standard varieties of English:

- Nominal plural with *them* (as is *dem boys* 'the boys')
- Copula absence (*Mary sick/ home*)
- Periphrastic marking of tense/aspect (unstressed habitual *do* and *does*, remote phase *been*, continuative *do/duh*, perfect *done* as in *Faye done go*)
- Invariant relativization with *what* (*everything what he say*)[12]
- Null complementizer (*You say Faye done gone*)
- Reported speech introduced by *say* (*I hear say Faye done gone*)

All this favours the view that creoles are natural languages deriving from non-standard varieties of certain European languages. There is no deviation or corruption in creoles; saying this would be tantamount to claiming that non-standard, colloquial varieties of European languages are deviations or corruptions of the corresponding standard written forms, a position that we can roundly reject. This point has been empirically confirmed on many occasions:

> Moreover, the language of the various corpuses of informal conversation is not degenerate. Occasionally speakers do make slips of the tongue, but only once in the 50,000 words of the Scottish English Corpus of spontaneous conversation is there a serious breakdown of syntax – interestingly, at a point where the speaker is trying to express a complex set of conditions by means of relatively complex syntax. (Miller and Weinert 1998: 383)

The idea that non-standard spontaneous language varieties are degenerations or corruptions of the corresponding written forms is one of the major tenets of the written languages bias in linguistics, described at length by Linell (2005). The same tenet is also a well established cultural myth of contemporary society, as Linell also notes:

> [T]he general point is that it is spoken language that deviates from written language, the latter being the implicit (or explicit) norm, rather than the other way around. As regards misunderstandings, and other failures of communication, these imperfections are due to mistakes and incompetencies residing in the communication individuals, since language in itself is, by definition, 'correct'. (Linell 2005: 57)

It is important to be aware of this myth, because sometimes creole languages are seen as the result of an imperfect or defective learning of a European language on the part of the slaves, due to a supposed incompetence and ignorance. Yet such a view is clearly little more than a new instantiation of the same myth. Creoles develop as the result of the natural laws of linguistic evolution based on non-standard varieties of European colonial languages. From this point of view, creoles are not deviational, corrupted or simple languages, but are completely normal natural languages. Of course, the majority of creoles have never been written or standardized. But these are cultural-dependent artificial developments, and, as defined in this essay, have to do with cultivated languages (E-languages).

Thus, as a general rule in linguistics, the everyday, normal speech used in informal conversations should constitute the fundamental basis on which a grammatical characterization of a language should be based, since it is this speech type that constitutes the main basis of natural language acquisition and the main manifestation of FLN (see Levinson 1983: 284).

5.3 Signed languages as natural languages

Recent developments in linguistics have led to a re-evaluation of signed languages, which can no longer be neglected in a serious study of the FLB and the FLN. They are not, as has commonly been believed in the past, secondary or surrogate with respect to spoken languages, and the present state of our knowledge concerning human language confirms beyond doubt that natural signed languages are direct manifestations of human FLN. Indeed, current theoretical linguistics has accommodated such a position in its fundamental statements and tenets. For example, the basic architecture of human language faculty has been characterized by Hinzen thus:

> A realm of sound, or gesture (as in sign languages), that the system has to equally interface with, else language could not be externalized (or be heard/seen). (Hinzen 2009: 126)

On this view, gesture, together with sound, is incorporated into the characterization of the human language faculty per se.

As discussed in Chapter 2, the evolution of human language supposes the emergence of a recursive combinatory system. This system seems to be modality-independent, as noted by Chomsky:

> If the relation to the interfaces is asymmetric, as seems to be the case, then unbounded Merge provides only a language of thought, and the basis for ancillary processes of externalization. There are other reasons to believe that something like that is true. One is that externalization appears to be independent of sensory modality, as has been learned from studies of sign language in recent years. (Chomsky 2009: 29)

If the externalization of language is a secondary process, then the modality of externalization and/or materialization is relatively independent of the core properties of FLN:

> There are independent reasons for the conclusion that externalization is a secondary process. One is that externalization appears to be modality-independent, as has been learned from studies of signed language in recent years. The structural properties of sign and spoken language are remarkably similar. Additionally acquisition follows the same course in both, and neural localization seems to be similar as well. That tends to reinforce that language is optimized for the system of thought, with mode of externalization secondary. (Berwick and Chomsky 2011: 32)

The fact that signed languages are spontaneously created, as is the case with natural spoken languages, is also symptomatic of the idea that the language faculty is modality-independent:

> Cases like Nicaraguan Sign Language and Al-Sayyid Bedouin Sign Language, perhaps more than spoken creoles since there cannot be any issue of substrate and superstrate influence, demonstrate beyond doubt that there is something to language acquisition that is more than just statistical correlation of inputs. Such cases indicate that the central question for cognitive scientists should no longer be whether there is a predisposition to grow a language (a term I prefer to 'language acquisition' because 'acquisition' suggests an E-language perspective, since it gives the impression of grabbing something outside one's brain), but rather, what this predisposition includes. (Boeckx 2010: 45)

Signed languages are traditionally seen as concerning manual gestures, and spoken languages as concerning vocal acoustic productions. On such a view, signed languages are gestural and are related to vision, whereas spoken languages are vocal and are related to audition. This would imply that these two language modalities are completely unrelated from the point of view of I-language externalization.

However, this is highly questionable. It should be noted first that non-vocal gestures, particularly manual gesticulation, play an important role in spoken language communication. The gesticulations accompanying speech usually play a paralinguistic function but in some cases can also have a purely linguistic one,[13] as in the following examples:

> *English sentences with gestural components*[14]
> a. The deaf person went _____ (speaker makes the appropriate gesture) yesterday.
> b. When the cop told her to leave, Sheila went ____ (speaker makes the appropriate gesture) (twice)

In both sentences here, a manual gesture plays a grammatical role as a verbal complement.

Yet there is a more fundamental sense in which it can be said that spoken languages are gestural in nature. It is not unreasonable to think of articulatory phonetics as concerning the coordination of certain gestures of the articulatory organs:

> We can think of the movements of our tongues and lips as gestures, much like the gestures we make with our hands. When we talk we use specific gestures, much like the gestures – controlled movements – to make each sound. (Ladefoged 2001: 3)

Indeed, Hale and Reiss (2008), in their critical overview of the practice of phonological analysis, speak about a *gestural score* mapping out the relative durational and dynamic properties of the intended articulatory target (Hale and Reiss 2008: 109). Some models of phonological analysis are in fact based on a gestural and dynamic view of phonetics and phonology. Browman and Goldstein (1992), for example, maintain that phonology is based on articulatory gestures which do not coincide with traditional phonemes, and that the phonological system privileges the syllable as the pattern of coordination among gestures.

As noted in Moreno Cabrera (2011), this gestural approach to phonology is not necessarily linked to articulatory phonetics. Models of speech perception exist which are based on dynamic sound patterns rather than on the static accumulation of constant phonological segments. For example, the multiple-trace model of memory (Hintzman, 1986, 1988; Taylor, 1997; Shockey, 2003, pp. 67–71) 'assumes that each experience produces a separate memory trace and the knowledge of abstract concepts is derived from the pool of episodic traces at the time of retrieval. A retrieval cue contacts all traces simultaneously, activating each according to its similarity to the cue, and the information retrieved from memory reflects the summed content of all activated traces responding in parallel' (Hintzman 1986: 411).

As a result, both spoken and signed languages are in themselves gestural languages. Hence, from the point of view of externalization both language modalities could share a common physiological basis. There is some neurological evidence in support of such an intimate relationship. It is generally accepted in contemporary neurological research that the perisylvian areas within the left hemisphere are involved in speech production and comprehension; these include the well-known Broca's and Wernicke's areas:

> A rough idea may have been selected as a symbol in the pre-frontal cortex and signalled to the automatic parts of language form organization, namely Broca's and Wernicke's areas. (Schnelle 2010: 45)

Broca's area is associated with the structuring of utterance production and Wernicke's area seems to serve sound pattern perception and the organization of grammatical structure (Schnelle 2010: 30). This has been confirmed by modern imaging studies:

> Imaging studies that monitor activity during different linguistics tasks consistently show activation of Broca's and Wernicke's areas of the cortex, as well as many other cortical areas. (Lieberman 2006: 196)

In her insightful overview of some psychological and neurological aspects of signed language research, Emmorey notes that injures in the perisylvian areas of the left hemisphere also provoke aphasia in users of signed languages:

> The data from adult signers who have suffered some type of brain injury clearly show that damage to perisylvian areas of the *left* hemisphere (the language zone) can cause frank sign language aphasias. (Emmorey 2002: 273)

Emmorey thus concludes that:

> The patterns of impairment that have been reported for sign aphasia are similar to what has been found for spoken language aphasia, indicating that there is a common functional organization for the two forms of language. Specifically, damage to anterior language regions causes nonfluent aphasias (e.g. Broca's aphasia), whereas fluent aphasias (e.g. Wernicke's aphasia) arise from lesions involving posterior language regions. (Emmorey 2002: 286)

She goes on to say that these findings could have a profound significance on the study of the language faculty:

> More striking, perhaps, is that the same neural structures (e.g. Broca's area, Wernicke's area) are engaged for the production and comprehension of both signed and spoken language. This neural invariance across language modalities points to a biological or developmental bias for these neural structures to mediate language at a more abstract level, divorced from the sensory and motoric systems that perceive and transmit language. (Emmorey 2002: 313)

In their overview of studies of signed language, Sandler and Lillo-Martin have also identified solid evidence for linguistically significant properties of signed languages (2006: 477–478):

- Signed languages distinguish between coordinated and recursively embedded sentences.
- Signed languages allow arguments of a verb to be covert provided that they are properly licensed.
- Signed languages have syntactic movement subjected to the same constraints found in spoken languages.
- Signed languages combine meaningful words with word partials to form more complex words.
- Signed languages make a clear distinction between morphological inflection and morphological derivation.
- Signed languages can present a systematic alternation of different forms for the same word partial (allomorphy).
- Signs are comprised of organized categories of distinctive features, and there are constraints on the ways in which these feature categories may combine.
- A syllable-like unit has been identified in signed languages.
- When word and word partials are combined, phonological alternations can occur.
- The phonology of signed languages segments and interprets utterances through a prosodic system with some characteristics that are comparable to those of spoken language.
- Signed languages present hierarchical organization in all their linguistic levels.

These many properties, taken together, seem to justify the idea that spoken and signed languages are two different modalities of the same type of natural language; indeed, they appear to belong to exactly the same linguistics species associated with *Homo sapiens sapiens*.

Having thus argued that signed and oral languages are two modalities of the same linguistic species, we might suspect that oral and signed language can undergo contact and mixing phenomena. But do signed and oral languages mix?

Before answering this question, several important distinctions must be clearly stated and properly understood, to avoid a great deal of misunderstanding and potential confusion. Apart from natural signed languages, two other systems of signing are used in communication between and with deaf people: fingerspelling and manual (artificial) sign codes (Deumert 2000: 423).

Fingerspelling represents the letters of a written language by means of certain manual configurations. For English there are two fingerspelling systems, British and American. Fingerspelling is often used in signed languages to spell out place names or proper names, and such a system is essentially a translation into manual signs of the written form of spoken languages. For this reason, they are culturally elaborated and are by no means universal.

Manual sign codes are artificially created for representing a spoken language visually and are used mainly in education. In these codes, signs from the national signed language are borrowed and are arranged according to the word order of the contingent spoken language and invented signs for inflections are added (Deumert 2000: 423). Consequently, these manual sign codes (usually called signed English, signed Chinese, etc.) are not natural languages, but rather highly standardized systems that must be consciously taught and learned. It is important to bear in mind, then, that these signed languages are not natural signed languages; instead, they originate as a visual elaboration of a spoken language intended for a specific purpose.

To return to the issue of contact situations involving (natural) signed and oral language, it must be borne in mind that most signed language users are bilingual:[15]

> [M]ost deaf individuals are bilingual even though they differ regarding their competence in and use of a signed language and a spoken/written language. The continuum of linguistic profiles encountered among deaf individuals ranges from mother tongue acquisition of one or both languages, the acquisition of one of the two languages as a second language, a partial acquisition of one or both languages to only a rudimentary acquisition of one or both languages. (Plaza-Pust and Morales-López 2008: 336).

As can be seen here, the availability for contact between a signed and a spoken language is in essence no different from that in the case of two spoken languages. Nevertheless, there are modality-dependent differences between the two types of contact. For example, simultaneity in the realization of sign and spoken languages[16] is an interesting differentiating factor:

> In a situation of contact involving a signed language and spoken language, in contrast, the possibility of a *simultaneous* production of elements of both languages is primarily related to their difference in modality: there is, in principle, no *articulatory* constraint that would impede the use of the two languages at the same time […]. (Plaza-Pust and Morales-López 2008: 356)

Instances of code-blending between sign and spoken languages have indeed been reported in the literature:

> In contrast to mixing that involves to spoken languages when the languages produced are a signed and spoken languages, these can be combined simultaneously in time. This simultaneity poses extra challenges to the analysis of bimodal mixing at many levels. In the Western sign languages studied thus far mixing appears to be frequent since the spoken language and the signed language are continuously in contrast with one another. (Baker and Van den Bogaerde 2008: 2)

The authors here studied a specific case of this type of code-mixing in the process of language acquisition:

> In the acquisition of Sign Language of the Netherlands (NGT) and spoken Dutch […], code-blending was also shown to occur to a considerable extent between deaf parents and their young children. (Baker and Van den Bogaerde 2008: 3)

This type of intermodal language mixing has also been observed in a study of language contact between Chinese Sign Language (CSL) and spoken/written Mandarin Chinese:

> During the interviews, many of my deaf interlocutors often signed CSL combined with lip movements (mouthing) representing the corresponding vocalizations of Chinese words. In this type of bimodal language mixing, the mouth expresses the syllabic information of a Chinese word supplemental to the respective sign producing the semantic information. […] In addition, the analysis of the data reveals that the signed element is used to ensure the understanding of the mouthed element, and the mouthed element is used to clarify the sign. Consequently, this type of mixing serves a pragmatic function: signers want to make sure their interlocutors understand the meaning of their message. (Yang 2008: 313)

The same author also observed code-mixing between CSL and signed Chinese:

> In our interviews, we observed that signers sometimes break down simultaneous or compound signs producing the individual morphemes separately, thus code-switching to signed Chinese. Indeed, I had the opportunity to observe code-switching between CSL and signed Chinese in both directions in the interactions of a mixed group of deaf and hearing individuals. For example, a CSL signer signed the negative hand-waving sign and the sign for 'know' in the Chinese word order, and then quickly switched to CSL and produced the compound sign KNOW-NOT for 'do not know something'. (Yang 2008: 315)

Contact between signed and spoken languages, then, is a very common phenomenon, and the two language modalities can interact with each other in complex ways in order to produce a special type of linguistic contact not known in the case of spoken languages. This is due to the fact that sign and spoken languages can be used simultaneously.

5.4 The revival of relativism[17]

It is not surprising that the central role that some modern traditions of linguistic research confer on the diversity of languages, and indeed the depth of this diversity, has led to a revival of linguistic relativism (e.g. Lucy 1992; Levinson 2003). We believe that the often unclear differentiation between the biological and cultural dimensions of language as outlined in our current essay is one of the main causes of this process.

Questions such as to what extent do the languages we speak determine how we see the world, how we think, and how we live our lives have always fascinated people, and have been addressed by a multitude of philosophers, anthropologists, linguists and psychologists.

Precisely because of the close attention it has received in various fields, linguistic relativity is not easy to define. Instead of trying to do so, we will characterize *linguistic neo-relativism* by citing the influential experimental psychologist Lera Boroditsky:

> Linguistic processes are pervasive in most fundamental domains of thought, unconsciously shaping us from the nuts and bolts of cognition and perception to our loftiest abstract notions and major life decisions. Language is central to our experience of being human, and the languages we speak profoundly shape the way we think,

> the way we see the world, the way we live our lives. (Boroditsky 2009: 129)

This strong relativistic statement has at least three related implications, all problematical: (i) if language influences thought, then language is different from thought; (ii) if languages influence the way we see the world, it is not our way of seeing the world that influences languages; and (iii) there is empirical evidence confirming the first two statements.

As regards the first implication, note that any question concerning the relationship of determination existing between language and thought necessarily implies previous definitions of *language* and of *thought*, yet such definitions are not to be found in the works that have addressed this issue, either past or present; this is of little surprise, since we simply lack such definitions. Of course it is entirely possible that language does not only influence thought, but that language is part of thought (see section 2.3.3). Even in such a case the relativist hypothesis is not necessarily correct, and is so only if language is identified with languages (i.e. in an inductive sense). Thus, from a point of view that the diversity among languages is relatively superficial (that is, confined to the manner in which homogeneous computational processes are externalized), the discovery that human thought makes extensive use of language does not in any way lead to the conclusion that human thought is fragmented into groups coinciding with languages. On the contrary, it would support the hypothesis that human thought is essentially homogeneous within the species. In fact, any theoretical model that accepts a certain degree of natural bias towards language acquisition should reject Boroditsky's relativist hypothesis.[18] Only a radically empiricist conception of the human mind and brain could accept that external cultural objects (human languages in the functional-cognitive paradigm) could 'profoundly shape the way we think'.

One can infer that Boroditsky (2009) and Deutscher (2010), to cite two recent writers of works of great social impact, accept that languages influence thought in that they operate with a rather vague notion of thought (and, obviously, because they believe in the myth of the diversity of languages, see 2.2.1). In a review of Deutscher (2010) published in *The New York Times* (5 September 2010), Derek Bickerton notes that the aspects of language Deutscher deals with 'do not involve "fundamental aspects of our thought", as he claims, but relatively minor ones'. Thus, Bickerton points to issues such as location, colour and grammatical gender (which are also the main topics dealt with experimentally by Boroditsky in support of her position), noting that they probably have little conditioning on our thought in the daily management of our lives, and even less in the development of political, scientific or philosophical thought.[19]

Let us address the second and third implications of the relativist hypothesis: that languages determine our way of seeing the world (and not vice versa), and that we have empirical evidence for this. Boroditsky in fact argues that, compared to discussions of the relationship between language and thought in the past, empirical work is currently being done that could resolve these ancient disputes. Specifically, she states that research conducted in her laboratories at Stanford and MIT has resulted in a large body of data from around the world (China, Greece, Chile, Indonesia, Russia and Aboriginal Australia), and that 'what we have learned is that people who speak different languages do indeed think very differently and that even flukes of grammar can profoundly affect how we see the world' (Boroditsky 2009: 118). This is not the place for a detailed review of the ingenious experiments and remarkable discoveries in this field of research, but it may be useful to consider, for example, what kind of experimental evidence supports the claim that 'flukes of grammar can profoundly affect how we see the world'.

Boroditsky (2009: 127) asks whether the fact that in Russian *chair* is masculine and *bed* is feminine makes Russian speakers think that in some way chairs are more like men and beds are more like women. Her conclusion is that this is indeed the case. In search for empirical to support such as assertion, Boroditsky and colleagues (Boroditsky *et al.* 2003) asked speakers of Spanish and German to describe (in English) objects which in these two languages have opposite gender (for example *key*, which is feminine in Spanish, *la llave*, and masculine in German, *der Schlüssel*). It was observed that Spanish speakers were more likely to use words like *golden, intricate, small, beautiful, bright* or *very small*, while the Germans tended to use more words like *hard, heavy, irregular, jagged* or *useful.*[20]

Regardless of the details of the experiment, and the criteria for determining which terms are more characteristic of men or women in certain societies, it does not seem to us that these findings show that the language we speak 'profoundly' determine our world view, but only that speakers of languages with masculine and feminine gender marking may be prone to extend sexual stereotypes to sexless objects, an extension based on the analogy of grammatical gender that is not available for English or Japanese speakers. We simply cannot infer from these experiments that a Spanish speaker conceives of the bridges in a 'profoundly' different manner than a speaker of German (or English). There do not appear, at least, to be any notable differences in the way bridges (or keys) are designed and built in Germany and Spain; in such tasks aspects of physics, engineering, strength of materials, economics and (of course) aesthetics come into play, and these do not seem to be grouped linguistically.

Of course, it is clear that languages interact with culture and that to a large extent are part of it. Another example discussed by Boroditsky and colleagues is the expression of space in languages, a topic addressed in depth by Levinson (2003). According to Boroditsky, speakers of Kuuk Thaayore (Pormpuraaw, Australia) do not express space in reference to an observer (left, right, front, back) but use the cardinal points (north, south, east, west). Hence it seems that when speaking a language in which one must say 'my west leg' instead of saying 'my left leg' it is essential that one always knows where west is. According to Boroditsky 'the result is a profound difference in navigational ability and spatial knowledge between speakers of languages that rely primarily on absolute references (like Kuuk Thaayorre) and languages that rely on relative reference frames (like English)' (Boroditsky 2009: 121). She goes on to claim that 'speakers of languages like Kuuk Thaayorre are much better than English speakers at staying oriented and keeping track of where they are, even in unfamiliar landscapes or inside unfamiliar buildings. What enables them – in fact, forces them to do this – is their language' (ibid.)

But if the 'cause' here is the language itself, one might wonder what is the cause of the situation in which in some languages people use 'left', 'right', 'in front' or 'behind' and in others they use 'east', 'west', 'north' or 'south'. It seems clear that the answer cannot be other than that the speakers of the second group pay much more attention to the cardinal points. The argument, then, is circular. At some point, certain aspects of the culture or lifestyle of people led to these decisions, so it is unclear how one might conclude that it is the language which influences the world view, and not the world view which influences the language.

All languages, especially in their lexicon, have a dimension which is sensitive to people's culture and lifestyle and, in effect, transmits culture and a view of life. A community in which the consumption of mushrooms is particularly prevalent is likely to have terms for many varieties of mushrooms, a richer lexicon in this respect than a language spoken by those living in places where mushrooms simply do not grow. But it would be unwise to say that having many words for different varieties of mushrooms causes a greater appreciation for this item of food itself.

To put it another way: when Deutscher and Boroditsky (following numerous authors) argue that languages determine or constrain our vision of the world, what they are really saying is that those parts of languages sensitive to culture determine or constrain our culture; this, indeed, is beyond dispute.[21]

Undoubtedly, good orientation in space is part of the culture or the lifestyle of the Kuuk Thaayorre. It is also clear that their culture has made their language (like those of other aboriginal Australians) express in this way both spatial location and, by analogy, temporal location. Indeed, this is shown in experiments that Boroditsky (2009) reviews, in which speakers of this language were asked to order drawings temporarily, and instead of doing so from left to right, they did it from east to west. But what the experiment really shows is not that language determines thought, but that Kuuk Thaayorre speakers are sensitive to their culture both when speaking and when performing certain experimental tasks.

Boroditsky formulates the key question as follows: 'are languages merely tools for expressing our thoughts, or do they actually shape our thoughts?' (Borodotsky 2009: 118). Note, however, that the alternative offered is too narrow, and effectively blocks a lot of options, which are discarded without consideration. In fact, as we have seen, we have every reason to believe that languages are not tools to express thoughts or shape our thoughts. One alternative is that languages are different externalizations, variable and historically conditioned, of a single system of knowledge. Certainly, it would be surprising that a computational system that allows us to create new expressions without theoretical limit, without scope restriction and free of conditioning stimulus (and which is at the heart of every human language), were not also involved in the way humans think about the world and try to understand it in a specifically human way, beyond evident (and interesting) cultural differences.

We have argued here, then, that psycholinguistic experiments designed to demonstrate the influence of languages on thought actually reveal that culture can affect languages. This latter point seems undeniable, in that languages are indeed important vehicles in the transmission of culture from one generation to another.

It could then be argued, however, that another path to linguistic relativism is thus opened up. If we apply the analogy with natural evolution, one might expect that languages somehow adapt to the worldview of their speakers, in the same way that organisms adapt to their environment. That is, we might expect some type of correlation between the structure of languages and the cultural environment in which they are spoken, which in turn would add weight to the relativist hypothesis.

It is true that natural organisms adapt to the environment, albeit in a blind and random manner. Consider a hippo or a whale. It is clear that they are adapted to live in the water, but only when compared with a cow or an antelope and not, for example, with a tench or a bluefin. The environment clearly influences the selection of variants, but it is difficult to delimit the extent of this. Speaking of culture, ideology or worldviews as adaptive frameworks of languages is too loose and general an approach.[22]

It is therefore likely that the effect of culture on languages is very limited, although superficially very visible. With regard to I-languages, the effect of culture (understood as the way of life, traditions and social, political and religious institutions of a human community) is limited to only those domains of I-languages that are not driven by naturally conditioned principles (be they 1 or 3 type factors), mainly in the sphere of lexicon and, of course, phraseology.

As regards the deepest aspects of the structure of languages, if they adapt to the environment, then we can conclude that the environment is nearly invariable. This would not be surprising if such an environment were mainly internal to the brain and mind. As pointed out by Pinker, there are languages in which the direct object follows the verb and languages in which it precedes the verb, but there are no left-object cultures and right-object cultures.[23]

In the review of Deutscher (2010) cited above, Bickerton offers an exaggerated (almost cartoonish) hypothetical correlation that, unlike the expression of space or morphological gender, would be directly relevant to the relativist hypothesis:

> Suppose relative clauses appeared only when a society entered the market economy. Any such finding would revolutionize our understanding of the interface between language and culture. But not only has no such relationship ever been demonstrated, nothing remotely like it has ever been found. (Bickerton, *loc cit.*)

We share this observation, but wonder if Bickerton has ever read Everett (2005).

Notes

1. More explicitly, Fitch adds the following: 'Nonhumans never do what every normal human child in the same situation will spontaneously do by the age of four: invent a wide variety of multi-word sentences that they have never heard but which are nonetheless "correct" and interpretable, and use these utterances to describe past and future (or imaginary) events, to ask questions, to describe their own wants and needs, and to ask others about theirs. It is this biological difference that we seek to understand, if we are to understand a critical aspect of human nature.' (Fitch 2010: 81)
2. This passage is quoted by Labov (2001: 9) when discussing the parallels between biological and linguistic evolution.
3. Pages 242 to page 321 include a description of the syntactic use of the verbal forms, and we have not included these pages in our page count.
4. Gil explicitly maintains that his analysis runs counter to the arguments put forward by Bisang, but he does not make the necessary points to demonstrate this.
5. As we have suggested in 3.3, other claims about the apparent extreme simplicity of certain aboriginal languages such as those maintained by Everett (2005) with respect to Pirahã are not borne out under close linguistic analysis.

6. See Cook and Newson (2007: 146–162) for a brief review and Pesetsky and Torrego (2011) for a brief updated survey.
7. Nevertheless, we consider interesting and worthy of careful study McWorther's hypothesis that the differences in the complexity of inflectional morphology (in terms of overspecification, irregularity and suppletion) in the grammars of languages is determined significantly by the extent to which second-language acquisition has played a role in the history of languages.
8. We have also echoed Sherman's observation that from a sufficiently abstract standpoint, there would be only a multicellular organism with surface patterns of variation, and have tried to show that this is the same for I-Languages (see 2.2.1) once we adopt a naturalistic stance.
9. The bonobo Kanzi is said to have acquired a considerable linguistic ability by using visual symbols known as lexigrams (Savage-Rumbaugh *et al.* 1998: 3–74). Although the authors claim that this visual communication system was learned spontaneously by Kanzi, it cannot be said that it is a natural communication system: the system is an invented language serving a specific purpose (communication between humans and bonobos), and as such meets neither the communicative necessities of humans nor those of bonobos.
10. See Kachru *et al.*, eds. (2006) for a comprehensive survey.
11. Data taken from Holm (1989: 405–551).
12. See Miller and Weinert (1998: 349) for examples of this construction in certain colloquial varieties of English.
13. See Moreno Cabrera (2011) for an overview.
14. Postal (2004: 184, 188).
15. This includes both deaf and hearing people. Hearing people who know a signed language are by definition bilingual.
16. Simultaneity also occurs within signed languages, since these languages have two main articulators (the two hands) that can act at the same time (see Vermeerbergen *et al.* (eds) 2007 for an overview). If we consider intonation and other supra-segmental features of spoken language, we might also see in these various layers of production some degree of simultaneity in articulation.
17. This section reproduces part of Mendívil-Giró (2012).
18. As Bolender notes, 'if some sort of Whorfian hypothesis turns out to be true, as these works suggest, this should not only mean that linguistic differences account for some cognitive differences. It should also mean that linguistic similarities account for some cognitive similarities across cultures. If linguistic differences so crucially enter into cognition, as a Whorfian would claim, it is unlikely that similarities would be cognitively irrelevant' (Bolender 2010: 2662).
19. Thus, Bickerton concludes in the aforementioned review: 'Moreover, with the possible exception of color terms, cultural factors seldom correlate with linguistic phenomena, and even when they seem to, the correlation is not causal'.
20. Another example used by the authors is *puente* ('bridge', masculine in standard Spanish) compared with *Brücke* (feminine in German), with similar

results. Interestingly, *puente* is a variable gender word in Spanish, being feminine in some dialects.

21. Boroditsky (2009: 124) asks 'how we do know that it is language itself that creates these differences in thought and not some other aspect of their respective cultures?' (2009: 124). Her answer is based on experiments in which English speakers are trained to express time, for example, as Greek speakers do, and once they are trained, they show that 'their cognitive performance began to resemble that of Greek (…) speakers' (2009: 124–125), which, according to Boroditsky, 'suggest[s] that patterns in a language can indeed play a causal role in constructing how we think' (ibid.). But note that assuming these individuals have changed their way of thinking implies a very vague and imprecise definition of 'thinking'. Likewise it could be argued that when the subjects are trained they acquire a new 'culture' that affects their performance. Boroditsky adds that 'in practical terms, it means that when you're learning a new language, you're not simply learning a new way of talking, you are also inadvertently learning a new way of thinking' (2009: 125), which in this context is the same as saying you are learning a new culture.

22. Even in the natural world the environment can be rather complex. If we think of a whale, water comes to mind, but if we think of a peacock, we find that its physical environment is not very useful in explaining its hypertrophic tail, unless we include peahens' mating preferences as part of their 'physical environment'. Peacocks' wonderful tails do not help them to nimbly escape predators or go unnoticed, but it seems that peahens select this kind of tail, perhaps through a simple attraction to it. Delimiting the environment for natural selection is not as easy as it seems, and the exercise is exponentially harder for 'linguistic selection'. The number of different factors that can affect the destiny of a linguistic variant is so complex and varied that the concept of adaptation to the environment ('culture') is simply not a concrete one.

23. 'One of the great findings of linguistics, vastly underappreciated by the rest of the intellectual world (and probably not highlighted enough by linguists themselves) is that the non-universal, learned, variable aspects of language don't fit into any meaningful, purposive narrative about the surrounding culture. Linguists have documented vast amounts of variation, and have a good handle on many of its causes, but the causes are internal to language (such as phonological assimilation and enhancement, semantic drift, and syntactic reanalysis) and aren't part of any symbolic or teleological plan of the culture.' (Steven Pinker, in http://www.edge.org/discourse/recursion.html)

6 Natural and cultivated languages: A necessary distinction

In this final section we will consider some of the consequences of the failure to make the distinction between natural (NL) and cultivated languages (CL). Most of the received ideas, prejudices and myths related to the analysis of human language may be attributed to a failure to distinguish clearly and analyse properly the natural and the social dimensions of language and their complex interrelations. Although most linguists claim that they are aware of, and reject, most of these prejudices, the fact remains, as we have seen in the preceding sections, that some aspects of them continue to find their way into the views of many scholars dealing with language and languages in contemporary society.

In the ten sections of this chapter we will state, respectively, ten well established linguistic facts arising from the current state of knowledge about the human language faculty, and we will see how a failure to make a clear distinction between NLs and CLs may contribute to these facts being questioned or rejected.

6.1 All human natural languages (spoken and signed) are direct manifestations of the human faculty of language

One of the main contentions of this essay arises from the observation that signed languages, as oral languages, are a direct manifestation of the human language faculty. Our present knowledge is not compatible with the idea that signed languages are language surrogates or in some way secondary with respect to oral languages. Signed languages have all the characteristics needed for a system of communication to qualify as a genuine direct manifestation of human FL. Every normal child can acquire naturalistically a signed language, given adequate exposure to it. This goes both for deaf and hearing children. One important feature of acquisition here is that whereas a deaf child cannot acquire a spoken language spontaneously, a hearing child can do so with any signed language to which he or she is exposed. Thus, from a linguistic point of view, signed languages are not exclusively the language of deaf people, and hearing people can also acquire or learn them. Social or educational reasons must, then, explain why most hearing people do not know a signed language. Of course, if most people knew a signed language, the social integration of deaf people would be much easier.

Evidence from biology supports this main contention. From a biological perspective, it is highly implausible to posit two different FLs, one for spoken languages and another for signed languages. The findings of contemporary studies of signed languages are consistent with only one FL, and do not support the idea that signed languages are derived in some way from spoken languages. There are signed spoken languages, but these are very different from natural signed languages and closer in many respects to spoken languages.

For many centuries, signed languages were not considered as full-fledged natural languages. They were viewed as imperfect substitutes for spoken languages, based on mimicking. In addition, since mimicking can be rather transparent and easy to understand, it was supposed, wrongly, that signed languages are understandable across the world, a kind of lingua franca of the deaf:

> There have been, and continue to be, a number of misunderstandings about sign languages. Some people see sign languages as grammarless attempts at communicating through gesture or pantomime. It is not uncommon for a relative or acquaintance to tell a hearing person learning a sign language how wonderful it must be to be able to communicate with people anywhere. Such statements are based on the misconception that sign languages are the same worldwide. The statements also contain a hint of the attitude that sign languages are understandable worldwide because they lack real language properties such as grammar, which would clearly differ from one language to the next. (Liddell 2003: 1)

Since mimicking is rather limited as a means of conveying complex and subtle messages, it was erroneously thought that signed languages were inferior to spoken languages and that deaf people could not communicate with each other and with the hearing people in a complete and efficient way:

> Naturally, such views and misunderstandings have social consequences. For example, some people might look down upon Deaf people, or even feel sorry for them, because they were limited to communicating through gestures rather than through language. (Liddell 2003: 2)

One of the first scholars who realized that signed languages are full-fledged natural languages was W. C. Stokoe. In 1957 he published *Sign Language*

Structure: An Outline of the Visual Communication Systems of the American Deaf, considered by many as the first demonstration that signed languages are genuine human languages. Yet his book was initially received with scepticism. As Liddell reports (2003: 4) the immediate response was 'Stokoe must be crazy!'

Almost 50 years after Stokoe's publication an influential monograph (Sandler and Lillo-Martin 2006) presented an impressive survey of the many findings of contemporary research in the field of sign linguistics. Its point of departure is eloquent indeed:

> Sign languages are conventional communication systems that arise spontaneously in all deaf communities. They are acquired during childhood through normal exposure without instruction. Sign languages effectively fulfil the same social and mental functions as spoken languages, and they can even be simultaneously interpreted into and from spoken languages in real time. (Sandler and Lillo-Martin 2006: XV)

The contention by Stokoe that signed languages are genuine natural human languages, then, has been confirmed by modern signed language research. There are many aspects in which both signed and spoken languages are alike but also many points in which they are different, sometimes very different. The similarities and differences between signed and spoken languages must be accounted for in any convincing theory of language, so the discussion of signed languages in theoretical linguistics should have a very significant influence on the development of the discipline. The crucial question in this respect is: in reality how similar are signed languages and spoken languages? One possible answer is the following:

> We think that the way to address this question is to take linguistic theory seriously, as a theory about universal properties of human language and to use it in the investigation of natural human languages in a different physical modality. (Sandler and Lillo-Martin 2006: XV)

From the above discussion it cannot be concluded that spoken languages manifest the human FL in its purest or fundamental form and that signed languages do so only in a more indirect or impure way. The great majority of research into human FL until now has been based on spoken languages.[1] This situation is circumstantial, a matter of prejudice about signed languages. Our present state of knowledge concerning signed languages does not support the maintenance of such prejudice.

6.2 All human natural languages (spoken and signed) belong to the same linguistic species

The idea that all human languages (spoken and signed) are essentially alike in their fundamental properties is one of the outstanding advances of contemporary linguistics. This property derives from the preceding assumption, above, and separates human languages from other types of communication used by other animal species. It can be said that for each biological species there is a distinct type of 'linguistic' system. Human language is associated with the *Homo sapiens sapiens* species as one of their peculiar and distinctive characteristics.

This does not mean that all natural languages are exactly alike. On the contrary, there is plenty of room for variation between any two human languages at each level of linguistic organization. But this variation is far from random, and is severely restricted in a number of significant ways.[2] The different linguistic types described in linguistic typology are different instantiations of a universal set of typological parameters characterizing all human languages.[3]

In order to establish a scientific basis for these observations a linguistic theory must be proposed and developed. The deepest unity of human natural languages must be accounted for in an ordered and inclusive way, and it seems to us that this can only be done by constructing a theory of human language using the hypothetico-deductive method, with hypotheses explicitly formulated and tested.

However, not all scholars agree with this procedure. Some propose that the methodology of linguistic science must be essentially inductive and particularistic, and thus genuine linguistic research does not need well developed theoretical apparatus. This point is made by Haspelmath in the following way:

> Framework-free grammatical description/analysis is argued here to be superior to framework-bound analysis because all languages have different categories, and languages should be described in their own terms. Frameworks represent aprioristic assumptions that are likely to lead to a distorted description of a language. I argue against restrictive theoretical frameworks of the generative type, against frameworks of functional approaches such as Functional Grammar and Role and Reference Grammar, and against Basic Linguistic Theory. (Haspelmath 2010: 341)

If this were true, each natural language would potentially correspond to a specific and unique type of linguistic knowledge. Each one of the human natural languages would have different properties and there would be no common human FL. Each human being would develop a unique and distinct type of ability corresponding to each different natural language; and these linguistic abilities would not have anything essential in common. In such a scenario no general language theory would be needed. The similarities between languages would be purely accidental, due to sheer chance; and the range of language variation would also be unlimited and random. Yet on this point of view it would be impossible to account for some of the most salient restrictions on language variation. For example, no known natural language orders the elements of a sentence according to the number of syllables in each word: for instance, first one syllable words, followed by two syllable words, three syllable words and so on.[4] Without a theory of human languages it would be impossible to explain this restriction and many others we could think of.

If we take seriously the idea that spoken and signed languages are genuine manifestations of the human FL, it is clear that we need a highly abstract linguistic theory. In order to characterize human FL correctly, we must make an abstraction of the differences between spoken and signed language, and hence current linguistic theory must be generalized in a number of significant ways. In contrast to Haspelmath's criticism, it is clear that we need a linguistic theory even more general and abstract than those normally used by linguists. This conclusion is inescapable if we maintain that there exists a human FL that distinguishes our species from other animal species.

As we have seen in section 5.2, any two human languages, no matter how different they seem, can give rise through mixing to a new human natural language. We have also seen that there can also be a very close relation between spoken and signed languages in this sense. A speaker can sign and speak at more or less the same time and different types of spoken/signed language mixing have been observed in the literature.[5] In fact, some authors have observed a total integration of a spoken and a signed language in linguistic performance:

> Phonological, morphological, syntactic, lexical and pragmatic features of two different languages are most often produced *simultaneously*, [so] assigning stretches of discourse to ASL or the English seems like a fruitless exercise and also misses the point. The point *is* [the creation of] a third system which combines elements of both languages and may also have some idiosyncratic data. (Ann 2001: 58–59). (Lucas and Valli 1992: 108)

This confirms the idea that spoken and signed languages belong to the same linguistic species. Otherwise it would be very difficult to account for such an intimate intermingling between, for instance, ASL (American Sign Language) and spoken English.

6.3 All known human languages are in the same stage of linguistic evolution

All known human languages (including those attested from the most remote points in time, such as Sumerian) are fully evolved. In prehistoric times, in which several hominid species coexisted, it is plausible that languages in earlier stages of linguistic evolution might have existed. But no such language has survived. If they did exist, then they disappeared together with the different hominid species that presumably used them. In addition, modern linguistic research has shown that creole languages are typical natural human languages, presenting a degree of grammatical development comparable to other natural languages not considered creoles. They cannot, then, be considered in any reasonable way as remnants of earlier stages of human language.[6]

If we consider spoken languages, the idea that there are more and less advanced languages from an evolutionary perspective was entertained in the nineteenth century, but contemporary linguistics gives us enough conceptual tools to set aside such a contention as unfounded.

The German linguist Schleicher distinguished isolating (Chinese), agglutinative (Turkish) and flexional languages (Greek, Sanskrit, Latin) and proposed that these three types represent three stages in human language development:

> Now according to Schleicher the three classes of languages are not only found simultaneously in the tongues of our own day, but they represent three stages of linguistic development. [...] The symbolic denotation of relation by flexion is the highest accomplishment of language. [...] But before a language can become flexional it must have passed through and isolating and an agglutinating period. (Jespersen 1922: 76)

This mistaken point of view, of course, is based on a particular understanding of language change. But language change is not language evolution. Natural languages do not change in order to evolve; on the contrary, they have evolved in order to change. Natural language variation and change are two of the main features of the already evolved human linguistic communication systems.

If we consider the changes from Anglo-Saxon to Contemporary English we see that a predominantly flexional language (Anglo-Saxon) has been transformed by the natural mechanisms of language change into a much more isolating language. But this has nothing to do with human language evolution: from an evolutionary point of view it is difficult to maintain the contention that Contemporary English is in some way more advanced than ancient Anglo-Saxon; both are full-fledged human natural languages.

We know that languages change over time, but we also know that these changes do not alter or modify the essential properties of human languages. Thus, languages attested from the earliest times are full-fledged natural languages, and present no primitive traits. Of course, it is possible that at some point in the history of humanity several precursors of current natural languages existed in the form of protolanguages[7] or pre-languages, truly primitive languages. But no attested human language has such a primitive status.

The failure to recognize the important differences between natural and cultivated languages leads many people to believe that written standard or literary languages must be viewed as evolutive developments of spontaneous spoken languages. The underlying idea here is that by elaborating these written versions, the many 'imperfections' and 'insufficiencies' of the spoken language are 'corrected' and as a result more 'perfect' languages are obtained. From this point of view Classical Latin is considered as a more developed language than Vulgar Latin, and Standard English is viewed as more perfect language that the many versions of spontaneous spoken English.

Classical Latin, Classical Greek, Sanskrit and Classical Arabic all present very complex and well developed orthography, pronunciation, grammar and vocabulary. From a strictly cultural perspective, they can be said to be more perfect, systematic, regular and coherent than the spoken languages on which they are based. Yet these culturally elaborated languages do not replace the corresponding natural spontaneous languages: the two forms of the language coexist, with the spoken form used by a majority of speakers, many of whom in fact never master the corresponding cultivated language, a fact observed by Dante several centuries ago. There is no evolutive transformation of a spontaneous spoken language into a classical written language. Cultivated languages are added to natural spontaneous languages as cultural elaborations. The idea that, through a generalized education, cultivated languages can replace natural spontaneous languages in the near proximate future is clearly a form of misplaced linguistic utopianism. Cultivated and written languages can of course influence in different ways the vocabulary and grammar of spontaneous spoken languages; for instance, many spoken languages present words coming from classical languages. But these influences do not alter in any significant way the fundamental linguistic laws determining the range and the limits of natural language variation and change. On the contrary, such influences are made possible only by those natural linguistic laws, permitting natural languages to respond and adapt in diverse ways to different environmental pressures.

6.4 Language change is not language evolution

All known natural languages change over time. This change has no evolutionary significance, inasmuch as it doesn't necessarily imply improvements or advances. Linguistic change does not transform a natural language into a new language in a more advanced evolutionary stage; as we argued in the preceding section, Modern English is not a more evolved language than Anglo-Saxon. Both are normal natural languages at exactly the same evolutionary stage.

In his essay on linguistic change *Linguistic Evolution*, Samuels gives the following proviso:

> Nevertheless 'evolution' is itself open to the misunderstanding that some sort of progress is implied, that a clearer or more effective means of communication has been achieved as a result of it. That meaning of 'evolution' is not intended here. We are not concerned here with the prehistoric origins of human language, and, as has often been pointed out, there is today no such thing as a 'primitive' language; every language is of approximately equal value *for the purposes for which it has evolved*, whether it belongs to an advanced or a primitive culture. (Samuels 1972: 1, quotation marks and italics as in the original)

It is usually assumed that languages change over time in the sense that a particular language is transformed and modified in certain specific ways by means of various processes of language change. This implies that languages are conceived of as objects subjected to modification and change as they are used by people to communicate to each other.

But this view seems plausible only in the case of cultivated languages, especially written ones. We can compare the written texts in English from different periods and observe linguistic changes in those texts. Indeed, there is a cultural literary tradition which renders plausible the idea that there exists a linguistic object called *the English language* that changes with time, and that changes are seen in the written texts from different periods. This view is rather superficial, since what in fact changes are not written texts in themselves but the grammatical rules that produce them:

> However, at this point it seems clear that the relevance of the individual text [...] to the enterprise is relatively marginal. One is

> not interested in the relationships between the linguistic texts of the *Fons* inscription, this particular letter from Cicero to Brutus, and the Strassbourg Oaths, but rather in the relationships holding between the grammars that produced these documents (which are assumed to stand in some kind of descent relationship with one another). (Hale 2007: 24)

This does not ignore the fact that there are secular cultural traditions involving different types of texts that we can trace and study from a philological perspective. But when we focus specifically on the linguistic aspects of those traditions, Hale's observation is absolutely right.

We have seen that cultivated languages are developed inside a certain cultural tradition that can be located at a specific time and can be studied as a more or less independent cultural concept. This gives rise to the idea that languages are cultural objects that can change with time.

If we focus on natural languages, it cannot be reasonably maintained that languages are historical objects that change over time. The reason for this lies in the fact that the transmission of spontaneous spoken languages is not continuous but discontinuous. Children do not acquire a natural language by copying the grammar of that language: they create a new linguistic competence based on the linguistic performance of the speakers/signers, since they cannot access the internal grammar (linguistic competence) of these speakers/signers. This situation differs in essential ways from the acquisition of the grammar of a written language. In this latter case, books exist which contain descriptions of the grammatical rules of written languages, to which both children and adults in general have direct access; such grammatical rules must be learned and used purposively in order to write, and possibly also speak, the cultivated languages.

The generational transmission of a natural language has a completely different character. Children have to build up their own grammatical rules, since they cannot access the inner linguistic competence of adults. From this it follows that natural languages are not transmitted at all; they are recreated by each new generation of speakers:

> It is apparent that language does not 'change' in the same sense as, e.g., the physical structure of the universe. In the latter case, we are dealing with the modification, under a variety of forces, of essentially the same substance over long periods of time. […] By contrast, in the case of language change, we must confront the fact that there is, in a very real sense, a different object (a different grammar) with each new generation. The grammar of my mother did not change into my grammar: I engaged in an ultimately successful process of grammar construction. This process of grammar

> construction gave rise to an entity in my brain, physically distinct from the entity in her brain, which underlies my first-language linguistic competence. (Hale 2007: 33)

Hale uses an illustrative metaphor for explaining this view. Language change cannot be described as a rock rolling down a hillside. A better metaphor requires some changes to this scenario:

> A large rock sits upon a hill. Every 20 years or so an individual with instructions to place and identical rock next to the rock they see on the hill comes along and does so. This individual is, however, barred from using anything other than visual inspection of the original rock to determine its features – they may not weight it, examine its internal structure, take measurements. […] These replacements proceed, at regular intervals, and 400 years later there is rock at the bottom of the hill which bears some resemblance to the original rock which sat at the top of the hill 400 years earlier. (Hale 2007: 34)

It is clear that in this scenario the original rock never rolled and that there are several rocks involved and not one rock. If such a metaphor is correct, it cannot be said that languages change. It makes no sense to say that Modern Greek comes from a series of transformations of Ancient Greek; what we have instead is a series of Greek languages created by each successive generation over many centuries.

If this approach is correct, there seems little point in inquiring whether languages improve or degrade over time, since languages are not transformed or changed at all. Each generation develops their own linguistic competence, driven by the properties of their natural FL, and in this sense each successive new language will be a new instance of human FL; therefore, no fundamental differences between these languages is expected to occur. Of course, this does not mean that the grammatical competences developed by children are exactly like those of adults. Differences may emerge that make these new competences innovative, producing thus a different natural language. The important thing here is that such innovations or changes do not affect the essential properties that characterize natural languages as manifestations of the human FL. So, these changes do not provoke any essential or fundamental changes that could modify or alter the nature of human languages. From this it clearly follows that natural language change does not produce more advanced or developed natural languages.

This is exactly what we observe in linguistic change. Modern Greek and Ancient Greek abide by the principles of human FL to the same extent and, therefore, it makes no sense to ask whether the modern language here is better or worse in some grammatical way than the ancient one.

From this point of view it makes no sense to speak about a long-term process of language transformation. The changes and adaptations of languages, through the creation of new grammatical competences by children, are restricted to a specific time and are completely independent of changes and adaptations that occurred in distant times. In this sense, all natural languages are new and the distinction between new and old natural languages makes no sense.[8] Haitian Creole and Modern Greek are two contemporary languages and it cannot be said that the second is older than the first: both had been created by modern generations of speakers. Of course it can be said that some form of Greek was spoken in ancient times; but this also can be said of Haitian Creole, since this language is distantly related to Latin via French.

Important differences also exist between Haitian Creole and Modern Greek. But these come from the corresponding cultivated languages. The Greek language has a long written tradition, whereas Haitian Creole does not. In this sense, it can be safely said that Haitian Creole is much more recent that Modern Greek. But this only as far as the cultivated versions of the two languages go.

As we have seen, the distinction between NL and CL is essential in order to make sense of several common ideas concerning the antiquity of languages and the nature and consequences of linguistic change.

6.5 All human natural languages (spoken and signed) present a similar degree of grammatical development

The notion expressed in the title of this section is an inescapable consequence of the ideas put forward in the preceding sections. For this reason all statements concerning the alleged grammatical superiority of certain languages over others must be viewed with suspicion. Frequently these statements are made on the basis of a superficial analysis of the languages involved, with analyses that evaluate the number of phonemes, morphological cases, verbal tenses or agreement types and then compare the figures obtained. For instance, if a language has five morphological cases and another language has 20, it is said that the first language is morphologically simpler that the second.

Yet this type of reasoning is profoundly flawed, since languages (or grammatical competences, to be more rigorous) are not constituted by a mere juxtaposition of a phonology, a morphology, a syntax and a semantics: there are also intricate interrelationships between all these components, in many cases unique to a particular language, and that in many cases are not well understood (or noticed at all) by linguists and grammarians.[9] For this reason, it makes no sense to compare the morphology of two languages in order to draw conclusions about their overall grammatical complexity. In fact, the morphology of each language interrelates with its other grammatical components in highly specific ways; thus, to compare the morphology of two different languages without also paying attention to their interrelations with the other components is of little use. Only by considering this integration we will obtain a more realistic and linguistically plausible comparison of languages. And for many languages this will lead to a much more complex view of their supposedly simple grammar.

However, at this point we must also take into account differences between NLs and CLs. As we have seen, it is only possible to speak of complex and simpler grammars if we focus on cultivated languages. Cultivated languages arise in a purposive and intentional way by means of a series of linguistic elaborations of the phonology, morphology, syntax and lexicon of a particular natural language. In a cultivated language new phonemes can be introduced, morphological paradigms can be regularized and generalized, new syntactic constructions can be integrated in the grammar, and the lexicon can be modified in certain ways: some lexical items can be replaced by others, the number of their readings can be diminished or expanded and so on. The more changes made to a natural language to obtain a cultivated language, the more difficult and complex that language will appear in the eyes of the corresponding natural language speakers. This is certainly the case with classical languages such as Classical Latin, Classical Arabic and Sanskrit. If we compare the grammar of these languages with the grammar of the natural languages on which they are based (Vulgar Latin, Vulgar Arabic and Prakrit) we can very easily draw the conclusion that the grammar of the classical languages is more complex, more perfect or more highly developed. Yet the fact remains that the grammar of these classical languages derives from a conscious elaboration of the grammar of the corresponding natural languages on which they are based. It makes sense to say that these classical grammars are more complex, regular and perfect because the grammar and lexicon of the corresponding natural languages have been subjected to a series of grammatical elaborations made by grammarians, poets or scholars who established a cultural tradition.

Such an assessment, though, concerns only cultivated languages, not natural languages. In this sense it is methodologically objectionable to compare the grammar of a cultivated language (for instance Classical Latin) with the grammar (grammatical competences) of a natural language (for instance, Vulgar Latin) and to draw conclusions concerning the complexity of that natural language. CL and NL are entities of disparate natures: they cannot be subjected to the same analytical criteria. To do so would be as senseless as comparing a rock with a sculpture made from stone. The sculpture is in some ways more complex that the rock; but this is so because the stone has been subjected to a purposive process giving rise to a work of art. It makes no sense to compare a rock with a stone sculpture in order to determine their ultimate or essential complexity. The rock's formation has to do with geology and with the laws of physics; the formation of the sculpture has to do with craftsmanship, art and human culture. Rock and sculpture, then, are objects of a very different nature; the stone sculpture, as a cultural object, has been obtained from a natural object (stone) and for this reason it is also subjected to the natural laws of geology and physics: the cultural elaborations of a stone cannot suspend or modify in any conceivable way these natural laws. On the contrary, the cultural elaborations of the stone to produce a work of art take advantage of the physical properties of the stone to produce the desired result.

Following this comparison, we can say that a natural language is the stone, and a corresponding cultivated language is the stone sculpture. The modifications made on the natural language to obtain a cultivated language can take advantage of the properties of the natural linguistic competences of the speakers/signers, but cannot go against the universal and fundamental proprieties of human FL characterizing natural grammatical competences. These modifications cannot alter or modify in any essential way these universal proprieties of human FL.

Comparisons between spoken and signed languages must also be made according to the preceding observations. In general, signed languages do not correspond to written languages, since those languages have not been submitted to the elaboration process typical of written standard languages. But in fact there are signed language elaborations used, for example, in signed poetry[10] and signed story-telling: these elaborations give rise to certain cultivated versions of signed languages that, as in the case of spoken languages, are based on the corresponding natural signed languages.

6.6 All human natural languages (spoken and signed) can be spontaneously acquired by human infants

Every human being is predisposed to acquire at least one natural human language in a spontaneous way. If a human being is exposed to both spoken and signed languages, he or she will acquire both languages. This observation is valid only for natural languages. Cultivated languages are in general not spontaneously learnable. They must be learned by means of a guided instruction; in industrialized societies children are typically taught a CL at school. In contrast to NL acquisition, CL learning is a purposive process requiring much attention and dedication on the part of the learner, as Dante noted several centuries ago. This is evident in the case of written language. The learning of reading and writing requires a continuous and strenuous effort and reading and writing skills must be cultivated throughout the life of the individual if a high degree of competence is to be achieved. Even in industrialized societies the notion of *functional illiteracy* (reading and writing skills that do not go beyond the most basic level) is also quite common. This contrasts with the ability of children to spontaneously acquire the phonological system of one or more natural languages, clearly a formidable task yet one that is fulfilled with complete success by every child, regardless of his or her overall intelligence. One specific aspect of this process is the segmentation problem of normal fluent speech:

> We suspect that newborn infants are even worse off than adults when it comes to perceiving fluent speech. Along with the other problems that stand in the way of speaking and understanding a native language, they must solve the segmentation problem for the first time. Moreover, they must do so with information-processing and memory resources that are less well developed than those of adults. Yet, since the overwhelming majority of infants learn to speak and understand a native language, they obviously do solve the segmentation problem and surmount all the other obstacles connected with learning a language. (Jusczyk 1997: 6)

Compared with this, the task of learning an alphabet seems much easier. But in spite of this, it is more difficult for a child to learn how to read and write that to learn how to understand and fluently speak a natural language. The reason for this paradox lies in the fact that the predisposition to acquire a phonological system or a gestural system is part of our faculty of language and children are naturally equipped to solve the formidable task of making linguistic sense out of the normal connected speech. By contrast, the ability to acquire reading and writing skills does not form part of our FL, since it is a cultural and not a natural linguistic phenomenon. For this reason, children require purposeful instruction if they are to fully acquire such abilities, and the results can vary greatly depending on the particular capabilities of the individual and the instruction received.

The comparison between the phonological systems of spoken natural languages and the different types of writing is very illustrative in this respect. All children acquire a natural language in more or less the same time period regardless of the complexity of the phonological system of their native language. For example, the phonological system of Polish (35 phonemes) can be judged in a first intuitive impression as much more complex than that of Spanish (25 phonemes),[11] yet Polish children do not take much more time than Spanish children to master the phonology of their respective languages.

As cultural developments, reading and writing skills develop in a completely different way. For instance, logographic writing is much more complex than alphabetic writing and hence mastering the Chinese or Japanese reading and writing takes in general far more time than mastering an alphabetic writing, both in the case of children and adult acquisition. Neither logographic nor alphabetic writing systems, though, can be spontaneously learned by children or adults.

6.7 All human natural languages (spoken and signed) are constrained in their competence and performance by the psycho-physiological limitations of human beings

Human natural languages are spontaneously used by human beings in everyday interaction. They are subjected to the physiological and psychical limitations and constraints of humans; the number of sounds the human vocal tract can produce and the number of manual signs that a human can perform are physically limited. The number of lexical items a human mind can store is also limited. Such constraints are valid for all humans and, consequently, for all natural languages.

The fact that CLs can escape the biological constraints of natural languages does not mean that communities using cultivated languages have overcome these limitations. Written languages do not operate under so many of these constraints. For example, multi-volume dictionaries and encyclopaedias can contain hundreds of thousands of words, far beyond the storing and processing capability of the normal human mind. But this fact does not affect in any fundamental way the manner in which people use their natural language in normal every day communication; in fact, the number of words used in normal, informal communication in a literate society is more or less the same as that used in similar situations in illiterate societies.

It could be argued that in more technologically advanced societies there is more vocabulary than in traditional societies, but this is clearly not the case:

> The fine detail and nuanced observation of Aboriginal vocabularies is so great that I will only have space to consider a few words of the natural world, though one could make similar points with terms for emotions, or smells and fragrances, or ways of moving. Many plant and animal species had distinct names in the Aboriginal languages in whose territories they are found well before they

> have been recognized as species by Western taxonomic biology. The *Oenpelli python*, for example, has had the long-established Kunwinjku name *nawaran* but was only identified as a distinct species in the 1960s, whereupon it received the Linnean name *Morelia oenpillensis*. (Evans 1998: 163).

Vocabularies differ depending on the type of society. An agricultural society will have a large vocabulary in matters related to land cultivation and husbandry; an urban society will have a relatively impoverished word stock in this regard but a much richer one relating to various urban matters. But the size of the commonly used vocabulary will be more or less the same, since this size is determined by the storing and processing capacities of our human brains. The same can be said of other levels of language structure. The linguistic sounds that a human being can produce and perceive are limited and these limitations are exactly the same for all physically normal human beings. This does not mean that all spoken languages have exactly the same linguistic sounds, but only that any human being can produce and perceive any sound of any human language. Some linguistic sounds, such as the click sounds of southern African languages, are sometimes said to be very difficult or impossible to pronounce by the non-native speakers of those African languages. But click sounds are in fact very easy to produce and indeed they are normally uttered as interjections with different uses by European people,[12] although not as phonemes.

6.8 E-Languages are not natural languages

E-languages as a set of products (sentences, texts, discourses), resulting from the natural linguistic activity generated by the grammatical competence and other types of cognitive and social procedures, are not natural languages at all, but cultural objects. Of course, these cultural objects can be studied and analysed in their own terms, but they do not constitute in themselves purely linguistic phenomena (that is, directly related to grammatical competences or I-languages).

One of the main contentions of certain current tendencies in linguistic analysis is the idea that a corpus of sentences, texts, discourses and conversations should always be the basis of serious theoretical linguistic research, most evident in the so-called corpus-based and corpus-driven analyses of language.[13] In corpus-based research actual texts or recorded speech are used in order to determine the systematic patterns of use governing the linguistic generalizations made by standard linguistic theory. This means that such theories have to do with linguistic performance and its products (conversations, oral discourses, written texts) and not with linguistic competence (the knowledge that makes possible the linguistic performance). Corpus-based research tends to formulate questions like the following: what is the more frequently used sentence type or tense used in casual conversation? What is the relative frequency of these sentence patterns in legal texts or in journalistic texts? The observation that relative clauses are more common in written texts than in informal conversation is one example of the findings of this type of research. All these investigations are very interesting and will help us to understand many aspects of linguistic performance in a particular community or society. But they do not concern the main goal of linguistic theory: the characterization of the specifically grammatical knowledge generating linguistic expressions. Thus, before determining the actual frequency of relative clauses in a specific type of discourse, it is first necessary to be aware of the grammatical patterns and generalizations giving rise to this type of subordinate clauses. In order to do so it is necessary to use the conceptual tools proposed in a particular grammatical theory; without such theoretical concepts it would be impossible to make sense of the raw data taken from real conversations, discourses or texts. The reason for this is very clear: these linguistic products are not only determined by linguistic generalizations but also by many different and disparate non-linguistic factors having to do with cultural traditions, ideology, social stratification, educational background and so on. The frequency of a particular sentence type in a particular speech register is controlled by the conjunction of many different social, ideological, cultural and educational factors. Of course, the study of these aspects of linguistic performance is very interesting in itself, but goes far beyond the realms of linguistics proper.

The goal of corpus-driven research is more relevant for linguistic theory in that it consists in discovering linguistic generalizations and categories not previously recognized by current theory. For example, thanks to a corpus of texts or recorded conversations certain word co-occurrences can be identified and described in statistical terms. Not all word combinations sanctioned by grammatical rules are equally frequent, with a great deal of variation in frequency, and such observations can suggest certain statistical patterns which are useful in describing and characterizing different discourse types in a linguistic community. All of this is very interesting in itself and worthy of study. But a linguistic theory is needed here as a starting point, in order that the relevant units to be submitted to a statistical analysis can be identified. In other words, it is clearly mistaken to believe that by looking in detail at linguistic corpora the rules of grammatical competence will immediately suggest themselves to us.

6.9 Only I-Languages are grammatical competences

When acquiring (or growing) a natural language, human beings develop a linguistic knowledge (linguistic competence) governing some aspects of their linguistic behaviour (linguistic performance). This linguistic knowledge in a person's mind is what Chomsky calls I-Language. It is not a directly observable entity and its properties can only be inferred from the study of the resulting use of that knowledge in linguistic production. But it is a mistake to view such production as the primary object of linguistic research. The primary object, rather, is a cognitive state of the human mind that makes such linguistic behaviour possible.

It has been argued that individual grammatical knowledge cannot be the real object of linguistic grammatical research, since we can access such knowledge only indirectly, by observing the linguistic performance of individuals. But this objection could also be levelled against much scientific enquiry. The laws of physics can only be observed in the behaviour of real objects in nature, yet real objects play no role in the formulation of the laws of physics: these are formulated in abstract mathematical terms and do not concern any particular natural object. Consider for example Archimedes' principle: 'The upward force exerted on a body immersed in a fluid is equal to the weight of the fluid the body displaces'. This principle involves a body and a fluid, but it would make no sense to ask: What particular body are we talking about? What real fluid are we talking about? The principle itself has, of course, arisen partly through experimenting with real objects in real fluids, but the corresponding physical law can only be stated in abstract terms concerning abstract bodies and fluids. The same applies to theoretical linguistic research: when we pose a grammatical rule establishing that a noun phrase consists of a determiner and a noun, the terms *determiner* and *noun* denote abstract categories known as grammatical classes in much the same way as *body* and *fluid* in Archimedes' law denote two kinds of physical objects.

It has also been argued that individual grammatical competences are in fact defective and partial instantiations of a more comprehensive inter-individual grammatical competence. Moreover, it is sometimes implicitly supposed that the only complete linguistic competence is that reflected in the grammar of a standard written language. But this view illustrates a failure to make the important distinction between NLs and CLs; it makes sense only for CLs such as written standard languages. These languages have an elaborated grammar based on a particular natural language: such grammatical elaborations can regularize, systematize or complete the grammatical competences characterizing a particular natural language. A cultivated artificial grammar is normally taught in a particular linguistic community and many individuals try to learn and use it properly. But, as we have seen above, when trying to use the learned grammar in everyday life people tend to naturalize it and therefore their linguistic performance shows an imperfect or defective realization of that standard language grammar. However, this occurs only in the case of CLs. The linguistic performance associated with natural linguistic competence, a natural language grammar, is not defective or imperfect[14] and it is not an implementation of a supra-individual grammatical competence, since such a competence simply does not exist. As we have argued in this essay, what we find is a population of natural grammatical competences that interact with each other and can experience processes of mutual adaptation or accommodation. But a population of grammatical competences is not a grammatical competence in itself, in the same way that a population of individuals is not an individual or a pack of wolves is not a wolf.

6.10 Cultivated languages are not natural languages

As we have seen in this essay, natural languages can be subjected to certain modifications serving particular purposes. These modifications can affect essential aspects of natural language and produce a new type of language: cultivated languages. Cultivated languages cannot replace natural languages since they lack some of their fundamental characteristics. In many Western societies such an attempted replacement has been tried for decades. Yet it is doomed to failure. Once a cultivated language is taught and put into practice, it becomes a natural language and loses some of the properties (stability, uniformity…) artificially concocted in the process of cultivated language elaboration. Written languages are the result of a conscious elaboration of a particular natural language, made by certain individuals and institutions.

CLs do indeed exist as a very special type of languages, and can be the object of scientific research, as can many other aspects of human society and culture. But although they are normally based on natural languages, they are not natural languages and, therefore, cannot be the primary scientific object of theoretical linguistics. In Europe, written languages such as Classical Greek or Classical Latin were for centuries considered the only full-fledged and complete languages, with vulgar vernaculars considered defective and incomplete; on this view, grammatical theory could only be established through the study of these classical written languages. The idea that only written languages have a grammar comes from this philological tradition and is maintained by some even today.

The development of modern theoretical linguistics has shown that this is wholly wrong. Modern linguistics has shifted the attention of scientific research in language from written languages to spontaneous spoken and signed languages, that is, to natural languages. One of the main points of modern linguistic research is that spontaneous spoken languages are not a defective or imperfect implementation of written standard languages. These latter languages are based on cultural elaborations of the former and they are to a lesser or greater extent artificial. This explains why non-educated speakers make mistakes when trying to speak a written standard language: they tend to naturalize that artificial language in order to make it adequate for normal everyday linguistic interaction, introducing a degree of variation and the under-determination typical of natural languages, but which is not permitted in cultivated languages. Cultivated languages can only be usefully described and studied when the corresponding natural languages on which they are based are taken as a reference. On the contrary, natural languages can be studied in themselves, without reference to their elaborated versions. Of course, in communities with a standard language tradition, some influence of the standard language on the spoken natural language can be expected; but this influence is superficial (predictably more intense in the lexicon and less so at other linguistic levels) and does not affect any essential features of the corresponding natural language. In addition, it must be pointed out that although many linguistic communities lack a standard written language, all human communities have one or more natural languages. So, the human FL manifests itself primarily in natural languages, and for this reason should be the primary scientific object of theoretical linguistic enquiry.

Notes

1. In some cases, in written versions of them.
2. Moro has referred to this as *the boundaries of Babel* (Moro 2008).
3. See Baker (2001) for an elementary overview.
4. This type of organization would be possible in a cultivated language. For example, in poetry there are severe constraints on the number and prosodic quality of the syllables that a particular type of verse may contain. But we maintain in this essay that cultivated languages are not natural languages.
5. See the discussion in section 5.3 of this book.
6. The idea that the grammar of creole languages is simpler or less developed than that of *normal* languages is based on prejudices and unproven assumptions, as has been brilliantly demonstrated by DeGraff (2001 and 2005); see the discussion in section 5.2 of the present book.
7. Bickerton (1990, 1995) and Arbib and Bickerton, eds (2010).

8. It only makes sense if we focus on cultivated languages developed by a long cultural tradition.
9. See Frajzyngier and Shay (2003) and Ramchand and Reiss, eds (2007) for an overview of the study of these interrelationships.
10. See for example Sutton-Spence (2005).
11. This figure corresponds to educated central-northern Castilian pronunciation, but if we consider the American Spanish varieties, 22 phonemes would be a more appropriate figure.
12. In both English and Spanish clicks are used as interjections to express disapproval or pity or to spur on a horse.
13. See Biber (2010) for an overview.
14. It can only be said to be imperfect or defective if we take into account the multiple extra-linguistic factors in linguistic performance that can distort the results of a natural grammatical competence.

References

Allan, K. (2007) *The Western Classical Tradition in Linguistics*. London: Equinox.

Alter, S. G. (1999) *Darwinism and the Linguistic Image*. Baltimore and London: The Johns Hopkins University Press.

Ann, J. (2001) 'Bilingualism and language contact'. In C. Lucas (ed.) *The Sociolinguistics of Sign Language*, 33–60. Cambridge: Cambridge University Press.

Arbib, M. A. and D. Bickerton (2010) *The Emergence of Protolanguage. Holophrasis vs Compositionality*. Amsterdam: John Benjamins.

Baker, M. (2001) *The Atoms of Language. The Mind's Hidden Rules of Grammar*. New York: Basic Books.

Baker, A. and B. Van den Bogaerde (2008) 'Code-Mixing in signs and words in input to and output from children. In Plaza-Pust and Morales-López (eds), 1–28.

Bathia, T. K. (2007) 'Bilingualism and Second Language learning'. In K. Brown (ed.) *Encyclopedia of Language and Linguistics*, vol. 2. London: Elsevier.

Benítez-Burraco, A. and V. M. Longa (2010) 'Evo-Devo – of course, but which one? Some comments on Chomsky's analogies between the biolinguistic approach and Evo-Devo', *Biolinguistics* 4 (4): 308–323.

Berwick, R. and N. Chomsky (2011) 'The biolinguistic program: The current state of its development'. In A. N. di Sciullo and C. Boeckx (eds) *The Biolinguistic Enterprise. New Perspectives on the Evolution and Nature of the Human Language Faculty*, 19–41. Oxford: Oxford University Press.

Biber, D. (2010) 'Corpus-based and corpus-driven analyses of language'. In Heine and Narrog (eds): 159–192.

Bichakjian, B. H. (2002) *Language in a Darwinian Perspective*. Frankfurt: Peter Lang.

Bickerton, D. (1990) *Language and Species*. Chicago, IL: Chicago University Press.

Bickerton, D. (1995) *Language and Human Behaviour*. London: UCL Press.

Bisang, W. (2009) 'On the evolution of complexity: sometimes less is more in East and mainland Southeast Asia'. In Sampson, Gil and Trudgill (eds) 2009: 34–49.

Bloomfield, L. (1933) *Language*, London: George Allen & Unwin.

Boeckx, C. (2010) *Language in Cognition. Uncovering Mental Structures and the Rules Behind Them*. Oxford: Wiley-Blackwell.

Boeckx, C. (2012) 'The I-Language mosaic'. In C. Boeckx, M. C. Horno-Chéliz and J. L. Mendívil-Giró (eds) *Language, from a Biological Point of View*, 23–51. Newcastle: Cambridge Scholars Press.

Boeckx, C. and K. K. Grohmann (2007) 'The Biolinguistics manifesto'. *Biolinguistics* 1: 1–8.

Bolender, J. (2010) 'Universal grammar as more than a programmatic label'. *Lingua* 120 (12): 2661–2663.

Boroditsky, L. (2009) 'How does our language shape the way we think?' In M. Brockman (ed.) *What's Next: Dispatches on the Future of Science*, 116–129. New York: Vintage Books.

Boroditsky, L. *et al.* (2003) 'Sex, Syntax, and Semantics'. In D. Gentner and S. Goldin-Meadow (eds): *Language in Mind: Advances in the Study of Language and Cognition*, 61–79. Cambridge, MA: MIT Press.

Botha, R. (2006) 'Pidgin languages as a putative window on language evolution'. *Language & Communication*, 26 (1): 1–14.

Briscoe, T. (2002) 'Introduction'. In T. Briscoe (ed.) *Linguistic Evolution Through Language Acquisition*, 1–22. Cambridge: Cambridge University Press.

Browman, C. and Goldstein, L. M. (1992) 'Articulatory Phonology: An overview'. *Phonetica* 49 (3–4): 155–180.

Burke, P. (2004) *Languages and Communities in Early Modern Europe*. Cambridge: Cambridge University Press.

Campbell, G. L. (1991) *Compendium of the World's Languages*. London: Routledge.

Chaudenson, R. (2003) *La Créolisation: Théorie, applications, implications*. Paris: L'Harmattan.

Chomsky, N. (1955) *The logical structure of linguistic theory*. Ms., Harvard University (Published partially in 1975, New York, Plenum).

Chomsky, N. (1981) *Lectures on Government and Binding*. Dordrecht: Foris.

Chomsky, N. (1986) *Knowledge of Language. Its Nature, Origins and Use*. New York: Praeger.

Chomsky, N. (1988) *Language and Problems of Knowledge. The Managua Lectures*. Cambridge, MA: The MIT Press.

Chomsky, N. (1995) *The Minimalist Program*. Cambridge, MA: The MIT Press.

Chomsky, N. (2000) *New Horizons in the Study of Language and Mind*. Cambridge: Cambridge University Press.

Chomsky, N. (2002) *On Nature and Language*. Cambridge: Cambridge University Press.

Chomsky, N. (2004) 'Beyond explanatory adequacy'. In A. Belletti (ed.) *Structures and Beyond*, 104–131. Oxford: Oxford University Press.

Chomsky, N. (2005) 'Three factors in language design'. *Linguistic Inquiry* 36 (1): 1–22.

Chomsky, N. (2007) 'Approaching UG from below'. In U. Sauerland and H.-M. Gartner (eds) *Interfaces + Recursion = Language? Chomsky's Minimalism and the View from Semantics*, Berlin: Mouton de Gruyter.

Chomsky, N. (2008) 'On phases'. In R. Freidin, C. Otero, and M. L. Zubizarreta (eds) *Foundational Issues in Linguistic Theory*, 133–166. Cambridge, MA: MIT Press.

Chomsky, N. (2009) 'Opening remarks'. In Piatelli-Palmarini, Uriagereka and Salaburu (eds), 13–43.

Chomsky, N. (2010a) 'Poverty of stimulus: Unfinished business'. Lecture presented in the Lecture Series 'Sprache und Gehirn – Zur Sprachfähigkeit des Menschen' organized by Angela D. Friederici in the context of the Johannes Gutenberg endowed professorship summer 2010.

Chomsky, N. (2010b) 'Some simple evo devo theses: How true might they be for language? In R. K. Larson, V. Déprez and H. Yamakido (eds) *The Evolution of Human Language. Biolinguistic Perspectives*, 45–62. Cambridge: Cambridge University Press.

Chomsky, N. and H. Lasnik (1993) 'The theory of principles and parameters. In J. Jacobs, A. von Stechow, W. Sternefeld and T. Vennemann (eds) *Syntax. An International Handbook of Contemporary Research*, 506–569. Berlin: Walter de Gruyter.

Comrie, B. (1992) 'Before Complexity'. In J. A. Hawkins and M. Gell-Mann (eds) *The Evolution of Human Languages*, 193–211. New York: Addison-Wesley.

Comrie, B. (2003) 'Reconstruction, typology and reality'. In R. Hickey (ed.) *Motives for Language Change*, 243–257. Cambridge: Cambridge University Press.

Comrie, B. and T. Kuteva (2005) 'Relativization strategies'. In Haspelmath, Dryer, Gil and Comrie (eds), 494–501.

Cook, V. J. and M. Newson (2007) *Chomsky's Universal Grammar. An Introduction*. (Third Edition). Oxford: Blackwell.

Coulmas, F. (1996) *The Blackwell Encyclopedia of Writing Systems*. Oxford: Blackwell.

Croft, W. (2000) *Explaining Language Change. An Evolutionary Approach*. London: Longman.

Darwin, C. (1871) *The Descent of Man, and Selection in Relations to Sex*. London: Penguin Books.

Dawkins, R. (1976) *The Selfish Gene*. Oxford and New York: Oxford University Press.

Deacon, T. W. (1997) *The Symbolic Species: The Co-Evolution of Language and the Brain*, New York: W.W. Norton.

Dediu, D. and D. R. Ladd (2007) 'Linguistic *tone* is related to the population frequency of the adaptive haplogroups of two brain size genes, *ASPM* and *Microcephalin*'. *PNAS*, 104 (26): 10944–10949 (Quoted from preprint version).

DeGraff, M. (1999) 'Creolization, language change, and language acquisition: A prolegomenon'. In M. DeGraff (ed.) *Language Creation and Language Change*, 1–46. Cambridge, MA: The MIT Press.

DeGraff, M. (2001) 'On the origin of creoles: A Cartesian critique of Neo-Darwinian linguistics'. *Linguistic Typology* 5 (2/3): 213–310.

DeGraff, M. (2005) 'Linguistics' most dangerous myth: The fallacy of Creole Exceptionalism'. *Language in Society*, 34 (4): 533–591.

Dennett, D. (1995) *Darwin's Dangerous Idea. Evolution and the Meanings of Life*. New York: Penguin.

Deumert, A. (2000) 'The sociolinguistics of Sign Language'. In R. Mesthrie, J. Swann, A. Deumert and W. L. Leap, *Introducing Sociolinguistics*, 419–448. Edinburgh: Edinburgh University Press.

Deutscher, G. (2010) *Through the Language Glass: How Words Colour your World*. New York: Metropolitan Books.

Dixon, R. M. W. (1997) *The Rise and Fall of Languages*. Cambridge: Cambridge University Press.

Dixon, R. M. W. (2002) *Australian Languages*. Cambridge: Cambridge University Press.

Eckardt, R., G. Jäger and T. Veenstra (eds) (2008) *Variation, Selection, Development. Probing the Evolutionary Model of Language Change*. Berlin: Mouton de Gruyter.

Ellis, N. C. and D. Larsen-Freeman (eds) (2009) *Language as a Complex Adaptive System*, Oxford: John Wiley & Sons.

Emmorey, K. (2002) *Language, Cognition and the Brain*. Mahwah, NJ: Lawrence Erlbaum.

Evans, N. (1998) 'Aborigenes Speak a Primitive Language", in L. Bauer and P. Trudgill (eds) *Language Myths*. London: Penguin Books.

Evans, N. (2010) *Dying Words. Endangered Languages and What They Have to Tell Us*. Oxford: Wiley-Blackwell.

Evans, N. and S. C. Levinson (2009a) 'The myth of language universals: Language diversity and its importance for cognitive science', *Behavioral and Brain Sciences*, 32 (5): 429–448.

Evans, N. and S. C. Levinson (2009b) 'With diversity in mind: Freeing the language sciences from Universal Grammar', *Behavioral and Brain Sciences*, 32 (5): 472–483.

Evans, N. and S. C. Levinson (2010) 'Time for a sea-change in linguistics: Response to comments on "The Myth of Language Universals"'. *Lingua* 120: 2733–2758.

Everett, D. L. (2005) 'Cultural constraints on grammar and cognition in Pirahã: Another look at the design features of human language'. *Current Anthropology* 46, 621–46.

Everett, D. L. (2007) 'Cultural Constraints on Grammar in Pirahã. A Replay to Nevins, Pesetsky, and Rodrigues', http://ling.auf.net/lingBuzz/000427

Fabb, N. (1997) *Linguistics and Literature: Language in the Verbal Arts of the World*. Oxford: Blackwell .

Fabb, N. (2002) 'Linguistics and literature'. In M. Aronoff and J. Rees-Miller (eds) *The Handbook of Linguistics*, 446–466. Oxford: Blackwell Publishing.

Fitch, W. T. (2009) 'Prolegomena to a future science of biolinguistics'. *Biolinguistics* 3 (4): 283–320.

Fitch, W. T. (2010) *The Evolution of Language*. Cambridge: Cambridge University Press.

Fitch, W. T., M. D. Hauser and N. Chomsky (2005) 'The evolution of the language faculty: Clarifications and implications'. *Cognition* 97 (2): 179–210.

Frajzyngier, Z. and E. Shay (2003) *Explaining Language Structure through Systems Interaction*. Amsterdam: John Benjamins.

Gell-Mann, M. (1992) 'Complexity and complex adaptive systems'. In J. A. Hawkins and M. Gell-Mann (eds) *The Evolution of Human Languages*, 3–18. New York: Addison-Wesley.

Gell-Mann, M. (1994) *The Quark and the Jaguar. Adventures in the Simple and the Complex*. New York: W. H. Freeman and Company.

Gil, D. (2009) 'How much grammar does it take to sail a boat?' In Sampson, Gil and Trudgill (eds) 2009: 19–33.

Givón, T. (2009) *The Genesis of Syntactic Complexity*. Amsterdam and Philadelphia, PA: John Benjamins.

Gould, S. J. (1996) 'The pattern of life's history'. In J. Brockman (ed.) *The Third Culture. Beyond the Scientific Revolution*, New York: Simon & Schuster.

Gould, S. J. (2002) *The Structure of Evolutionary Theory*. Cambridge, MA and London: Harvard University Press.

Greenberg, J. H. (1957) 'Language and evolutionary theory'. In J. Greenberg, *Essays in Linguistics*, 56–65. Chicago, IL: The University of Chicago Press.

Greenberg, J. H. (1959) 'Language and evolution'. In *Evolution and Anthropology: A Centennial Appraisal*, 61–75. Washington, DC: The Anthropological Society of Washington [reprinted in *Language, Culture, and Communication: Essays by Joseph H. Greenberg*. Stanford, CA: Stanford University Press, 1971, 106–125].

Greenberg, J. H. (1992) 'Preliminaries to a systematic comparison between biological and linguistic evolution'. In J. A. Hawkins and M. Gell-Mann (eds) *The Evolution of Human Languages*,139–158. New York: Addison-Wesley.

Hale, M. (2007) *Historical Linguistics. Theory and Method*. Oxford: Blackwell.

Hale, M. and Ch. Reiss (2008) *The Phonological Enterprise*. Oxford: Oxford University Press.

Harris, M. (1998) *Good to Eat. Riddles of Food and Culture*. Long Grove, IL: Waveland Press.

Harris, R. (1995) *Signs of Writing*. London: Routledge.

Harris, R. (2000) *Rethinking Writing*. London: Continuum.

Haspelmath, M. (2008) 'Parametric versus functional explanations of syntactic universals'. In T. Biberauer (ed.) *The Limits of Syntactic Variation*, 75–107. Amsterdam: John Benjamins.

Haspelmath, M. (2010) 'Framework-free grammatical theory'. In B. Heine and H. Harrog (eds) *The Oxford Handbook of Linguistic Analysis*, 341–366. Oxford: Oxford University Press.

Haspelmath, M., M. S. Dryer, D. Gil and B. Comrie (eds) (2005) *The World Atlas of Language Structures*, Oxford: Oxford University Press.

Hauser, M. D., N. Chomsky and T. Fitch (2002) 'The faculty of language: What is it, who has it, and how did it evolve?' *Science* 298: 1569–1579.

Hawkins, J. A. (2004) *Efficiency and Complexity in Grammars*. Oxford: Oxford University Press.

Heath, J. (1985) 'Discourse in the field: Clause structure in Ngandi'. In J. A. Nichols and A. C. Woodbury (eds) *Grammar Inside and Outside the Clause. Some Approaches to Theory from the Field*, 89–112. Cambridge: Cambridge University Press.

Heine, B. and T. Kuteva (2007) *The Genesis of Grammar*. Oxford: Oxford University Press.

Heine, B. and H. Narrog (eds) (2010) *The Oxford Handbook of Linguistics Analysis*. Oxford: Oxford University Press.

Hewitt, B. G. (1987) *The Typology of Subordination in Georgian and Abkhaz*. Berlin: Mouton de Gruyter.

Hintzman, D. (1986) 'Schema abstraction in a multiple-trace memory model'. *Psychological Review* 93 (4): 411–428.

Hintzman, D. (1988) 'Judgments of frequency and recognition memory in a multiple-trace memory model'. *Psychological Review* 95 (4), 528–551.

Hinzen, W. (2009) 'Hierarchy, merger, and truth'. In Piatelli-Palmarini, Uriagereka and Salaburu (eds), 123–141.

Hinzen, W. (2011) 'Language and thought'. In C. Boeckx (ed.) *The Oxford Handbook of Linguistic Minimalism*, 499–522. Oxford: Oxford University Press.

Holm, J. (1989) *Pidgins and Creoles. Volume II. Reference Survey*. Cambridge: Cambridge University Press.

Hualde, J. I. and J. Ortiz de Urbina (2003) *A Grammar of Basque*. Berlin: Mouton de Gruyter.

Hurford, J. R. (1992) 'An approach to the phylogeny of the language faculty'. In J. A. Hawkins and M. Gell-Mann (eds) *The Evolution of Human Languages*, 273–303. New York: Addison-Wesley.

Hurford, J. R. (2002) 'Expression/induction models of language evolution: Dimensions and issues'. In T. Briscoe (ed.) *Linguistic Evolution Through Language Acquisition*, 301–344. Cambridge: Cambridge University Press.

Isac, D. and C. Reiss (2008) *I-Language*. Oxford: Oxford University Press.

Ithurry (1895) *Grammaire Basque. Dialect Labourdin*. Bayonne: A. Lamaignère.

Jespersen, O. (1922) *Language. Its Nature, Development and Origin*. London: George Allen & Unwin.

Jespersen, O. (1933) 'Nature and art in language'. In *Selected Writings of Otto Jespersen,* 705–724. London: George Allen & Unwin 1960.

Joos, M. (ed.) (1957) *Readings in Linguistics*. Washington, DC: American Council of Learned Societies.

Jusczyk, P. W. (1997) *The Discovery of Spoken Language*. Cambridge, MA: The MIT Press.

Kachru, B. B., Y. Kachru and C. L. Nelson (eds) (2006) *The Handbook of World Englishes*. Oxford: Blackwell.

Kauffman, S. A. (1993) *The Origins of Order. Self-organization and Selection in Evolution*. London: Oxford University Press.

Keller, R. (1990) *Sprachwandel: Von der unsichtbaren Hand in der Sprache*. Tübingen: Francke.

Kirby, S. (1999) *Function, Selection, and Innateness. The Emergence of Language Universals*. Oxford: Oxford University Press.

Koerner, K. (ed.) (1983) *Linguistics and Evolutionary Theory. Three Essays by August Schleicher, Ernst Haeckel, and Wilhelm Bleek*. Amsterdam and Philadelphia, PA: John Benjamins.

Kusters, W. (2003) *Linguistic Complexity. The Influence of Social Change on Verbal Inflection*. Utrecht: LOT.

Labov, W. (2001) *Principles of Linguistic Change. Social Factors*. Oxford: Blackwell.

Ladefoged, P. (2001) *Vowels and Consonants. An Introduction to the Sounds of Languages*. Oxford: Blackwell.

Larsen-Freeman, D. and L. Cameron (2008) *Complex Systems and Applied Linguistics*. Oxford: Oxford University Press.

Lass, R. (1997) *Historical Linguistics and Language Change*, Cambridge: Cambridge University Press.

Law, V. (2003) *The History of Linguistics in Europe. From Plato to 1600*. Cambridge: Cambridge University Press.

Lepschy, G. (ed.) (1994) *History of Linguistics. Vol II. Classical and Medieval Linguistics*. London: Lonhman.

Levinson, S. C. (1983) *Pragmatics*. Cambridge: Cambridge University Press.

Levinson, S. C. (2003) *Space in Language and Cognition: Explorations in Cognitive Diversity*. Cambridge: Cambridge University Press.

Liddell, S. K. (2003) *Grammar, Gesture and Meaning in American Sign Language*. Cambridge: Cambridge University Press.

Lieberman, P. (2006) *Toward an Evolutionary Biology of Language*. Cambridge, MA: The Belknap Press of Harvard University Press.

Lightfoot, D. (1999) *The Development of Language. Acquisiton, Change and Evolution*. Oxford: Blackwell.

Lightfoot, D. (2006) *How New Languages Emerge*. Cambridge: Cambridge University Press.

Linell, P. (2005) *The Written Language Bias in Linguistics. Its Nature, Origins and Transformations*. London: Routledge.

Longa, V. M. and G. Lorenzo (2012) 'Theoretical linguistics meets development: Explaining FL from an epigeneticist point of view'. In C. Boeckx, M. C. Horno-Chéliz and J. L. Mendívil-Giró (eds) *Language, from a Biological Point of View*, 52–84. Newcastle: Cambridge Scholars Publishing.

Longobardi, G. (2003) 'Methods in parametric linguistics and cognitive history'. *Linguistic Variation Yearbook* 3: 101–113.

Lorenzo, G. (2012) 'The evolution of the Faculty of language'. In C. Boeckx, M. C. Horno-Chéliz and J. L. Mendívil-Giró (eds) *Language, from a Biological Point of View*, 263–289. Newcastle: Cambridge Scholars Publishing.

Lucas, C. and C. Valli (1992) *Language Contact in the American Deaf Community*. San Diego, CA: Academic Press.

Lucy, J. (1992) *Grammatical Categories and Thought: A Case Study of the Linguistic Relativity Hypothesis*. Cambridge: Cambridge University Press.

Maas, U. (2009) 'Orality versus literacy as a dimension of complexity'. In Sampson, Gil and Trudgill (eds), 164–177.

Manjón Pozas, F. J. and J. D. Luque Durán (1997) 'Aspectos lingüísticos e ideológicos en la valoración de la diversidad y perfección de las lenguas del mundo'. In J. A. De Molina Redondo and J. D. Luque Durán (eds) *Estudios de lingüística general II*, 202–222. Granada: Método Ediciones.

Marcus, G. F. (2006) 'Cognitive architecture and descent with modification'. *Cognition* 101: 443–465.

Matthews, P. (1994) 'Greek and Latin linguistics'. In G. Lepschy (ed.) (1994), vol. II: 1–133.

Mayr, E. (1942) *Systematics and the Origin of Species from the Viewpoint of a Zoologist*. New York: Columbia University Press.

McWhorter, J. H. (2001) 'The world's simplest grammars are creole grammars'. *Linguistic Tyology*, 5 (2/3): 125–166.

McWhorter, J. H. (2011) *Linguistic Simplicity and Complexity. Why do Languages Undress?* Boston, MA and Berlin: Gruyter Mouton.

Mendívil-Giró, J.-L. (2006) 'Language and species. Limits and scope of a venerable comparison'. In J. Roselló and J. Martín (eds) *The Biolinguistic Turn. Issues on Language and Biology*, 82–118. Barcelona: Universitat de Barcelona.

Mendívil-Giró, J.-L. (2009) *Origen, evolución y diversidad de las lenguas. Una aproximación biolingüística*. Frankfurt: Peter Lang.

Mendívil-Giró, J.-L. (2012) 'The myth of language diversity'. In C. Boeckx, M. C. Horno-Chéliz and J. L. Mendívil-Giró (eds) *Language, from a Biological Point of View*, 85–133. Newcastle: Cambridge Scholars Publishing.

Miller, J. and R. Weinert (1998) *Spontaneous Spoken Language*. Oxford: Oxford University Press.

Milroy, J. and L. Milroy (1991) *Authority in Language*. London, Routledge.

Mithun, M. (1999) *The Languages of Native North America*. Cambridge: Cambridge University Press.

Moreno Cabrera, J. C. (2000) *La dignidad e igualdad de las lenguas*. Madrid: Alianza Editorial.

Moreno Cabrera, J. C. (2008) 'The written language bias in linguistic typology'. *Cuadernos de Lingüística* XV, 117–137. Madrid: Instituto Universitario Ortega y Gasset.

Moreno Cabrera, J. C. (2011) 'Speech and gesture: An integrational approach'. *Language Sciences*, 33 (4): 615–622.

Moro, A. (2008) *The Boundaries of Babel. The Brain and the Enigma of Impossible Languages*. Cambridge, MA: The MIT Press.

Morpurgo-Davies, A. (1998) *Nineteenth-Century Linguistics* (vol. IV of G. Lepschy (ed.) *History of Linguistics*). London: Longman.

Mufwene, S. (2002) 'Competition and selection in language evolution'. *Selection*, 3 (1): 45–56.

Mufwene, S. (2008) *Language Evolution. Contact, Competition and Change.* London: Continuum.

Müller, M. (1862) *Lectures on the Science of Language.* New York: Charles Scribner.

Murelli, A. (2011) *Relative Constructions in European Non-Standard Varieties.* Berlin: De Gruyter Mouton.

Narita, H. and K. Fujita (2010) 'A naturalist reconstruction of minimalist and evolutionary biolinguistics'. *Biolinguistics* 4 (4): 356–376.

Nettle, D. (1999) *Linguistic Diversity.* Oxford: Oxford University Press.

Nevins, A., D. Pesetsky and C. Rodrigues (2009) 'Piraha exceptionality: A reassessment'. *Language* 85 (2): 355–404.

Newmeyer, F. J. (1998) *Language Form and Language Function.* Cambridge, MA: The MIT Press.

Newmeyer, F. J. (2005) *Possible and Probable Languages. A Generative Perspective on Linguistic Typology.* Oxford: Oxford University Press.

Nichols, J. (1992) *Linguistic Diversity in Space and Time.* Chicago, IL: University of Chicago Press.

Penn, D. C., K. J. Holyoak, and D. J. Povinelli (2009) 'Universal grammar and mental continuity: Two modern myths', *Behavioral and Brain Sciences*, 32 (6): 462–464.

Pesetsky, D. and E. Torrego (2011) 'Case'. In C. Boeckx (ed.) *The Oxford Handbook of Linguistic Minimalism*, 52–72. Oxford: Oxford University Press

Pettersson, J. S. (1996) *Grammatological Studies: Writing and its Relation to Speech.* Uppsala: Department of Linguistics.

Piatelli-Palmarini, M., J. Uriagereka and P. Salaburu (eds) (2009) *Of Minds and Language. A Dialogue with Noam Chomsky in the Basque Country.* Oxford: Oxford University Press.

Pietroski, P. M. (2011) 'Minimal Semantic Instructions'. In C. Boeckx (ed.) *The Oxford Handbook of Linguistic Minimalism*, 472-498. Oxford: Oxford University Press.

Pinker, S. (1994) *The Language Instinct. How the Mind Creates Language.* Cambridge, MA: The MIT Press.

Pinker, S. and R. Jackendoff (2009) 'The reality of a universal language faculty'. *Behavioral and Brain Sciences*, 32 (5): 465–466.

Plaza-Pust, C. and E. Morales-López (eds) (2008) *Sign Bilingualism. Language Development, Interaction, and Maintenance in Sign Language Contact Situations.* Amsterdam: John Benjamins.

Plaza-Pust, C. and E. Morales-López (2008) 'Sign bilingualism. Language development, interaction, and maintenance in sign language contact situations'. In Plaza-Pust and Morales-López (eds), 333–379.

Postal, P. M. (2004) 'The openness of natural languages'. In P. M. Postal *Skeptical Linguistic Essays*, 173–204. Oxford: Oxford University Press.

Radford, Andrew *et al.* (1999) *Linguistics. An Introduction.* Cambridge: Cambridge University Press.

Ramchand, G. and Ch. Reiss (eds) (2007) *The Oxford Hanbook of Linguistic Interfaces.* Oxford: Oxford University Press.

Ritner, R. K. (1996) 'Egyptian writing'. In P. T. Daniels and W. Bright (eds) *The World's Writing Systems*, 73–83. Oxford: Oxford University Press.

Ritt, N. (2004) *Selfish Sounds and Linguistic Evolution. A Darwinian Approach to Language Change.* Cambridge: Cambridge University Press.

Rooryck, J., N. V. Smith, A. Liptak and D. Blakemore (2010) 'Editorial introduction to the special issue of *Lingua* on Evans & Levinson's "The myth of language universals"'. *Lingua* 120 (12): 2651–2656.

Rosenbach, A. (2008) 'Language change as cultural evolution: Evolutionary approaches to language change'. In Eckardt, Jäger and Veenstra (eds), 23–74.

Rothstein, S. and A. Treves (2010) 'Computational constraints on compositional interpretation: Refocusing the debate on language universals'. *Lingua* 120 (12): 2717–2722.

Sampedro, J. (2002) *Deconstruyendo a Darwin. Los enigmas de la evolución a la luz de la nueva genética*. Barcelona: Crítica.

Sampson, G., D. Gil and P. Trudgill (eds) (2009) *Language Complexity as an Evolving Variable*. Oxford: Oxford University Press.

Samuels, M. L. (1972) *Linguistic Evolution with Special Reference to English*. Cambridge: Cambridge University Press.

Sandler, W. and D. Lillo-Martin (2006) *Sign Language and Linguistic Universals*. Cambridge: Cambridge University Press.

Saussure, F. de (1916) *Course de linguistique générale*. Paris: Payot (quoted from 1995 edition, Payot et Rivages, Paris).

Savage-Rumbaugh, S., S. G. Shanker and T. J. Taylor (1998) *Apes, Language and the Human Mind*. Oxford: Oxford University Press.

Sapir, E. (1921) *Language. An Introduction to the Study of Speech*. San Diego, CA: Harcourt Brace & Company.

Sherman, M. (2007) 'Universal genome in the origin of metazoa: thoughts about evolution'. *Cell Cycle*, 6 (15): 1873–1877.

Schleicher, A. (1863) *Die Darwinsche Theorie und die Sprachwissenschaft*. Weimar: H. Böhlau (Quoted from the 1869 English version *Darwinism Tested by the Science of Language* by J. C. Hotten, included in Koerner (ed.), 1–71).

Schnelle, H. (2010) *Language in the Brain*. Cambridge: Cambridge University Press.

Shockey, L. (2003) *Sound Patterns of Spoken English*. Oxford: Blackwell.

Sigurdhsson, H. A. (2011) 'On UG and Materialization'. *Linguistic Analysis* 37 (3–4): 367–388.

Smith, K. and Kirby, S. (2008) 'Natural selection for communication favors the cultural evolution of linguistic structure'. In A. D. M. Smith, K. Smith and R. Ferrer i Cancho (eds), *Proceedings of the 7th International Conference (EVOLANG7)*, 283–290. World Scientific.

Smith, N. (1999) *Chomsky: Ideas and Ideals*. Cambridge: Cambridge University Press.

Steels, L. (1997) 'Synthesising the origins of language and meaning using coevolution, self-organisation and level formation'. In J. Hurford, C. Knight and M. Studdert-Kennedy (eds) *Evolution of Human Language*. Edinburgh: Edinburgh University Press.

Sutton-Spence,R. (2005) *Analysing Sign Language Poetry*. Houndmills: Palgrave Macmillan..

Taylor, J. R. (1997) 'Linguistic theory and the multiple-trace model of memory'. In G. Wolf and N. Love (eds) *Linguistics Inside Out. Roy Harris and his Critics*. Amsterdam: John Benjamins: 208–225.

Tomasello, M. (2009) 'Universal grammar is dead'. *Behavioral and Brain Sciences*, 32 (5): 470–471.

Uriagereka, J. (1998) *Rhyme and Reason: An Introduction to Minimalist Syntax*. Cambridge, MA: The MIT Press.

Vermeerbergen, M., Leeson, L. and O. Crasborn (eds) (2007) *Simultaneity in Sign Languages. Form and Function*. Amsterdam: John Benjamins.
Wilcox, S. and P. Wilcox (2010) 'The analysis of signed languages'. In B. Heine and H, Harrog (eds.): 739–760.
Yang, Y. H. (2008) 'Sign language and oral/written language in deaf education in China'. In Plaza-Pust and Morales-López (eds), 297–332.
Yelle, R. A. (2006) 'Ritual and religious language'. In K. Brown (ed.) *Encyclopedia of Language and Linguistics*, vol. X, 633–640. London: Elsevier.
Zubiri, I. and E. (2000) *Euskal gramatika osoa* [A comprehensive Basque grammar]. Bilbao: Didaktiker, SA.

Index of Names

Index of Subjects

Index of Languages

www.ingramcontent.com/pod-product-compliance
Lightning Source LLC
LaVergne TN
LVHW010348080826
844660LV00003B/222
9781781790526